Editor

Lori Kamola, M.S. Ed.

Managing Editor

Karen Goldfluss, M.S. Ed.

Editor-in-Chief

Sharon Coan, M.S. Ed.

Illustrator

Ken Tunell

Cover Artist

Wendy Roy

Art Coordinator

Denice Adorno

Imaging

James Edward Grace

Product Manager

Phil Garcia

Many pages taken from
Extension Activity Book Series,
Teaching Spice, and *Thinking
Skills Series*
Publisher:
Blake Education

Publisher

Mary D. Smith, M.S. Ed.
Americanized Edition

Brain Puzzlers

Fun Thinking Games and Activities to be Done Independently

Ages 8–12

Contributing Authors

Rosalind Curtis, Maiya Edwards,
Jean Haack, Fay Holbert,
Sharon Shapiro, Timothy Tuck

Teacher Created Resources, Inc.

6421 Industry Way
Westminster, CA 92683
www.teachercreated.com

ISBN: 978-0-7439-3354-4

©*2002 Teacher Created Resources, Inc.*

Reprinted, 2008

Made in U.S.A.

Table of Contents

Table of Contents (cont.)

Table of Contents *(cont.)*

Brain Workouts

Math

Table of Contents *(cont.)*

Table of Contents *(cont.)*

Table of Contents *(cont.)*

Brain Challenges

Math

Table of Contents *(cont.)*

Table of Contents *(cont.)*

Introduction

Today's children are the problem solvers of the future. Children need many opportunities to explore creative solutions to problems and unfortunately, many activity books for children ask questions with only one right answer or that can be answered without much thought put into the process. This book is a compilation of creative, fun, and unique activities for children to complete independently. This book is divided into three sections, *Brain Warm-ups, Brain Workouts,* and *Brain Challenges*, progressing from easier activities to more challenging ones. Within each section are four categories: Math, Word Activities, Writing, and Creative Thinking. While the first three of these categories are often thought of as basic skills, in this book, the activities all emphasize creative thinking strategies. Some of the activity pages are word puzzles with a twist: each asks a question that is solved with the help of a clue or some scrambled letters after the rest of the activity has been completed. Other activities include math word problems that encourage drawing pictures to help solve the question. On other pages, children are given a creative writing prompt and encouraged to write and illustrate a story. Many pages are fun thinking skills activities asking children to create new objects or change and improve objects and explain their thinking. All children can learn to think more critically and creatively. A foundation in creative thinking skills will enable children to pursue lifelong learning.

•••••••••••••••••••••••••••• What is a Thinking Skill? ••••••••••••••••••••••••••••

In addition to helping us think clearly, thinking skills help us critically and creatively collect information to effectively solve problems. As a result of learning thinking skills, children will also become more aware of decision-making processes.

Improved thinking encourages children to look at a variety of ideas, search to greater depth, practice more critical decision making, challenge accepted ideas, approach tasks in decisive ways, and search for misunderstandings, while keeping the aims of the task clearly in mind.

The end results will be decisions that are more reliable, deeper understanding of concepts, contributions that are more creative, content that is examined more critically, and products that are more carefully created.

•••••••••••• Why do Children Need to Develop Thinking Skills? ••••••••••••

Children need to develop the abilities to judge, analyze, and think critically in order to function in a democratic and technological society. A family should value the development of thinking skills and provide opportunities for these processes to be modeled and developed. Thinking skills can be taught, and all students can improve their thinking abilities. Creativity is present in children regardless of age, race, socioeconomic status, or different learning modes.

The basic skills are generally thought of as reading, writing, spelling, and math. These processes involve computation, recall of facts, and the basic mechanics of writing. Of course, parents should want their children to master basic skills, but the learning process should not stop there. Frequently, children are faced with tasks that expect them to demonstrate their ability to use higher level thinking without having had the opportunities to develop their abilities with these thinking processes.

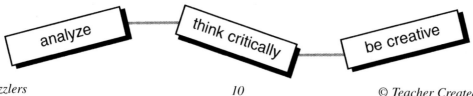

Introduction *(cont.)*

It is desirable to develop different thinking domains, as they have different aims and develop different skills:

♦ *Critical thinking* examines, clarifies, and evaluates an idea, belief, or action's reasonableness. Students need to *infer, generalize,* take a *point of view, hypothesize,* and find *temporary solutions.*

♦ *Brainstorming, linking ideas, using analogies, creating original ideas, organizing information,* and looking at a problem from *different perspectives* will lead to alternative solutions useful in decision making and problem solving.

♦ The *collection, retention, recall,* and *use of information* when needed is another vital skill.

♦ *Creative thinking* develops original ideas.

•••••••••••••••••••••• **Thinking Processes** ••••••••••••••••••••••

Eight processes, categorized into cognitive and affective abilities, have been identified as being important in fostering thinking skills:

Cognitive (thinking) Abilities

Fluency allows as many ideas as possible to be thought of by children.

Flexibility helps children look at problems from different perspectives and think of ways to combine unusual ideas into something new and different. At times, objects may have to be grouped according to different criteria.

Originality involves producing unusual or unique ideas.

Elaboration involves adding or further developing ideas.

Affective (feeling) Abilities

Curiosity involves working out an idea by instinctively following a pathway.

Complexity involves thinking of more complex ways of approaching a task. This may involve searching for links, looking for missing sections, or restructuring ideas.

Risk-taking is seen in children who guess and defend their ideas without fear that others will make fun of their thoughts.

Imaginative children can picture and instinctively create what has never occurred and imagine themselves in other times and places.

Introduction *(cont.)*

Parents can help their children learn thinking skills in a variety of ways. There are many questions that parents can ask of themselves:

☆ Do our children have opportunities to work on problems where creative thinking is valued?

☆ Are they encouraged to apply history's lessons to today's problems?

☆ Are they involved in planning family outings that will satisfy the needs of all family members?

☆ Are they allowed to participate in family projects such as redesigning rooms?

☆ Most importantly, are children allowed to be different?

☆ Are they listened to, even if their ideas are unusual or impractical?

☆ Are they reassured that, even if they are disagreed with, their ideas and input are valuable?

☆ In terms of the family as a whole, are they encouraged to be part of an environment where it is acceptable to make mistakes?

☆ Is the focus on learning from our children?

Introduction *(cont.)*

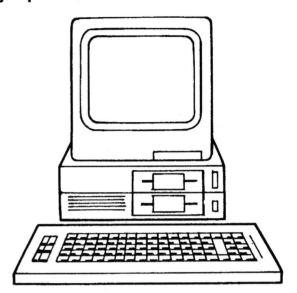

•••••••••••••••••••••••• Technology Tips ••••••••••••••••••••••••

Computer skills can be integrated into many aspects of the learning experience. Computer technology is useful for programming and problem solving. Spreadsheets and databases can develop higher order thinking skills and lateral thinking. They will also develop spacial orientation. Computer games can be used to motivate students and encourage task commitment. When software is carefully selected, it can be used to develop higher-order thinking skills. Simulation or strategy software is motivational and open-ended and involves players in critical thinking, risk taking, and real-life problem solving.

•••••••••••••••••••••••• Assessment ••••••••••••••••••••••••

Many pages in this book have open-ended answers; no one correct answer is required. For the pages with concrete answers, an answer key is provided at the back of the book. These pages are not meant to be graded; the answer key is provided for self-checking of answers. Many of the pages in this book ask thought-provoking questions, stimulating the children to think creatively and use their imaginations. Children can work on the activities at their own rate; a progress chart is included for children who like to keep track of the activities they have completed. A parent or other adult might choose to mark the progress chart with a sticker or a stamp after the activities have been completed to reward the child for a job well done. There are many options of stickers that can be purchased through Teacher Created Resources, some that might work well are TCM#1929, TCM#1990, TCM#1989, and TCM#1982. Also provided are some awards in the back of the book that parents can fill out and give when their children complete several of the activity pages. Children often enjoy devising their own problem-solving techniques; space is provided on the activity pages for children to explain how they arrived at their answers.

Brain Warm-ups

How Many?

1. A farmer has 12 sheep and 15 cows. How many animals does the farmer have altogether?

2. If a school has 12 classes and there are 25 students in each class, how many students are there altogether?

3. How many different ways can you show the number 285? Show 10 ways.

Representing Numbers

We can represent the number 12 using pictures and number sentences.

12 ✲✲✲✲✲✲✲✲✲✲ ✲✲ 10 + 2	12 ✳✳✳✳ ☆☆☆☆ ✳✳✳✳ 4 + 4 + 4

Think of two more ways to represent the number 12.

12	12

Use pictures and numbers to represent the numbers 11, 15, and 18 in as many different ways as you can.

11	15	18

Train Games

Draw a train like the one shown using cylinders of different sizes.

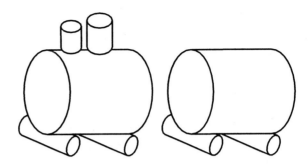

How many cylinders make up your train?

On the Beat

Out on the beat at 7 A.M., Police Officers Betty and Bernice pick up a trail. A brazen thief has stolen multiples of seven! Fortunately, the thief has dropped some along the way. So follow the trail until you exit the city block— and catch the thief!

	↓							49	
	7	21	49	70	77	50	14	56	
49	15				28			70	
	35	84	42	48	35	70	84	23	77
				20			21		70
49	14	63	56	42			14		56
	17			35	29	22	35	42	55
	77			56		48		49	70
	35	27	35	77	35	28			77
			48			14	7	14	28

Figure-Eights

Complete the figure-eight circuit by solving the problems below.

Across

1. 43 − 15

2. 9 x 2

3. 39 + 26 + 20

Down

1. 76 ÷ 2

2. 11 x 8

3. 100 − 11

4. 21 + 27

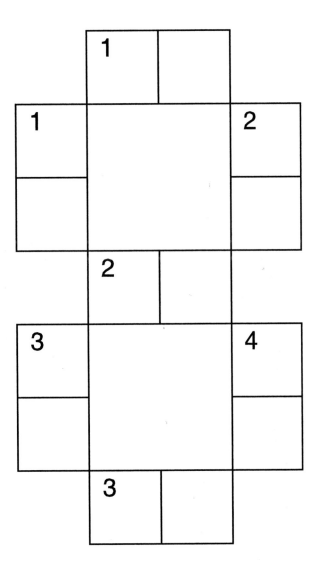

Travel Around the Island

Juan flew around the island in 95 hours. But which route did he take? Start from 'M' on the map and fly west to "A", then continue around the island. Your flight must take exactly 95 hours.

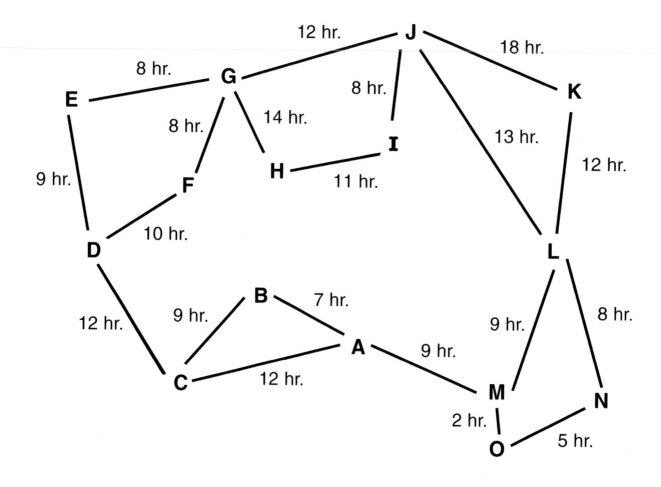

List the order of Juan's flight: _____

_____

_____

_____

A Grave Set of Sums

Starting with 12, write the answer to each math problem in the next circle. If you return to the top with the answer of 12, you've worked them all correctly!

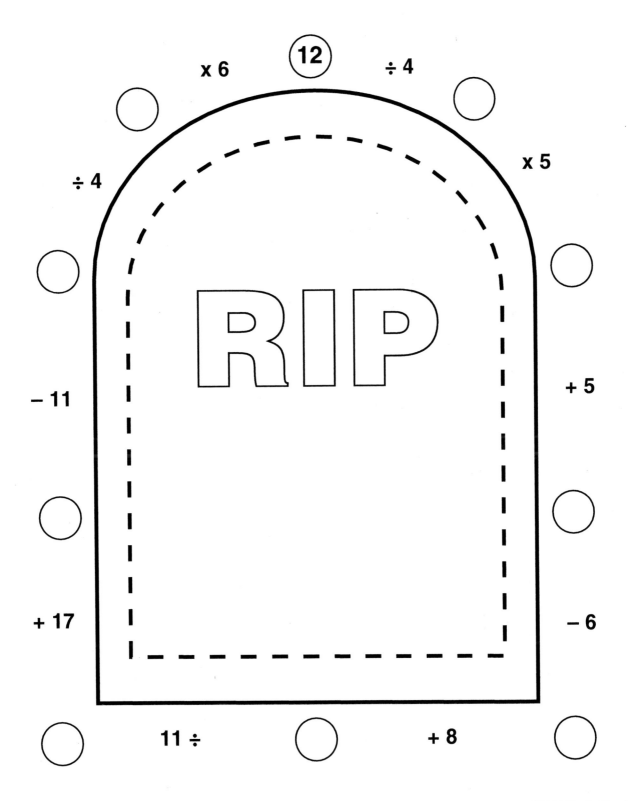

Tunnel Vision

George is stuck in another tunnel. The best way out is the one where he passes the smallest total, adding up the numbers as he goes. Can you find the best way for George to get out of the tunnel? Show your work.

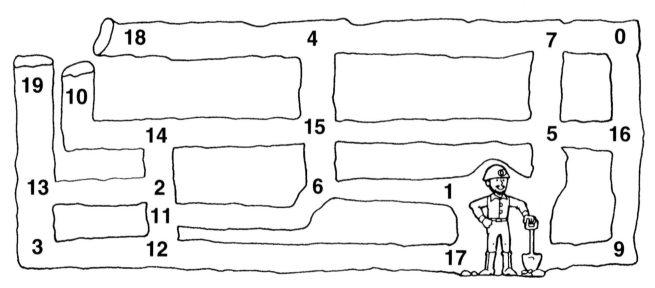

Roll 'em, Roll 'em, Roll 'em

The early stagecoach drivers were not very accurate when they were drawing their maps. This one certainly was not drawn to scale! The stagecoach needs to figure out how to get to town using the shortest route. The driver cannot tell which route is the shortest by looking at the map. Add up the miles between the towns to figure out which of the three routes (A, B, or C) is the shortest.

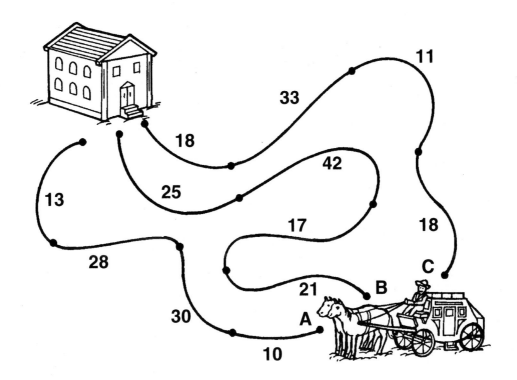

Which route should the stagecoach take? _____

What Comes Next?

Draw the next shape in each series.

1.	○ □ □ ○ □ □ ○ □	
2.	♡ △ △ ♡ △ △ ♡ △	
3.	○ ☆ ○ ☆ ○ ☆ ○ ☆	
4.	□ □ □ D D D ♡ ♡	
5.	○ △ ○ ▽ ○ △ ○ ▽	
6.	≡ ☆ □ ≡ ☆ □ ≡ ☆	
7.	□ △ △ ♡ ♡ ♡ D D D	
8.	△ △ ○ ○ △ △ □ □ △	
9.	♡ ♡ ☆ ♡ ♡ □ ♡ ♡ ☆ ♡	
10.	□ ▭ □ ▭ □ ▭ □ ▭ □	

Picture Shapes

Find the triangles and circles in the picture. Color the picture.

These things have △s:

These things have ◯s:

How Many Triangles?

How many triangles are in the picture? Count them and then color the picture.

There are _____ triangles.

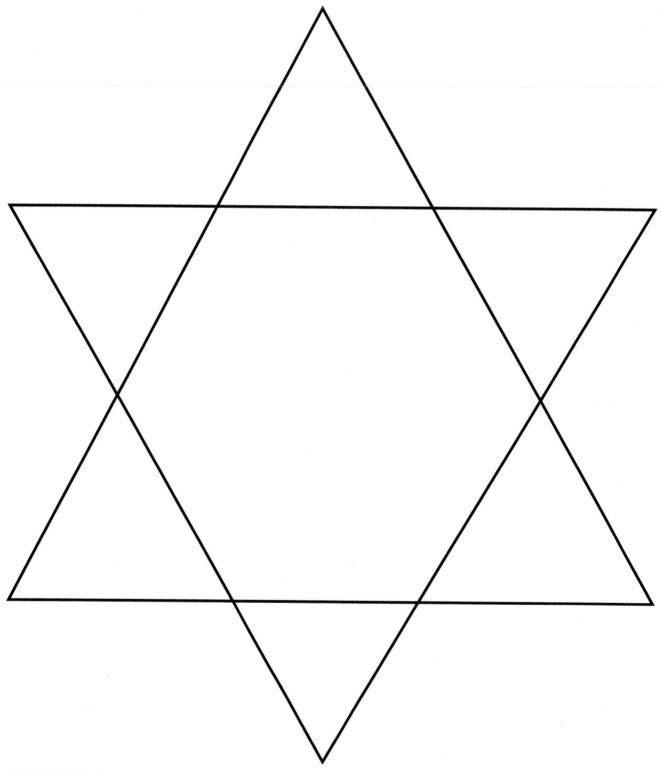

26

Color This Design

Color this design so that no shapes of the same color touch one another. You may use only three colors. (*Hint:* Think about the design before you begin to color.)

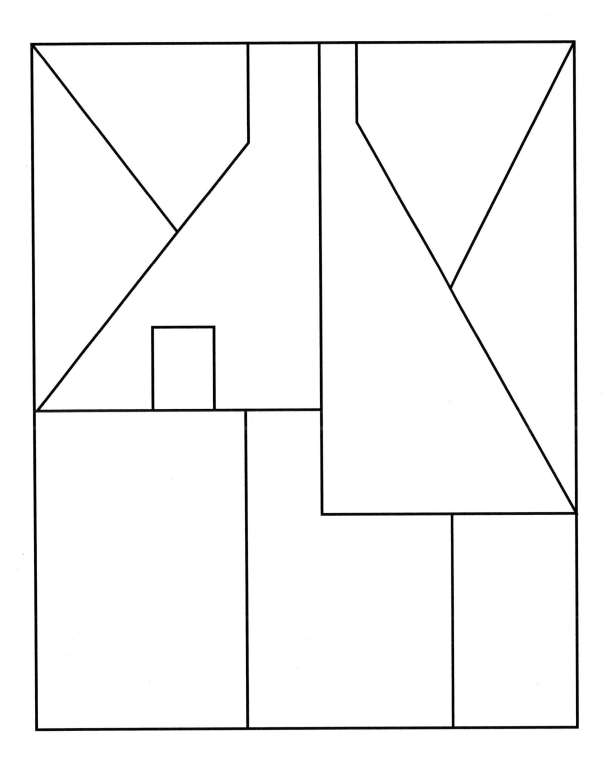

Addition and Subtraction Word Problems

Read the following problems. Circle the important facts you need to solve them. Use the space provided to find the solution to each problem.

1. There were 76 students in a school jog-a-thon. Twenty-six of them were in 3rd grade, 28 of them were in 4th grade, and 22 of them were in 5th grade.

   a. How many 4th and 5th-grade students were in the jog-a-thon?

   _____

   b. Which grade had the most students in the jog-a-thon? _____

2. The jog-a-thon route covered 150 kilometers. There were four rest stops for the runners. Niki ran 52 kilometers and stopped at the second rest stop.

   a. How much further does Niki have to run to complete the route?

   _____

   b. Has she gone at least half the distance? _____

Addition and Subtraction
Word Problems *(cont.)*

Read the following problems. Circle the important facts you need to solve them.
Use the space provided to find the solution to each problem.

3. Melita's team wanted to collect a total of $325.00. They collected
$208.75 from the jog-a-thon and $76.20 from a candy sale.

a. How much money did they collect? _____

b. Would they collect more money from three candy sales than from
one jog-a-thon? _____

4. Twenty team members had lunch together at the third rest stop.
They had traveled 70 kilometers. Thirteen team members drank milk
with their lunches and the rest drank grape juice.

a. How many team members drank grape juice? _____

b. How many students did not drink milk or grape juice? _____

Addition and Subtraction
Word Problems *(cont.)*

Read the following problems. Circle the important facts you need to solve them. Use the space provided to find the solution to each problem.

5. Bill, Holly, and Katie collected contributions from their neighbors. Bill collected $13.78, Holly collected $16.85, and Katie collected $12.34.

   a. How much more did Holly collect than Bill? _____

   b. How much did Holly and Katie collect together? _____

6. To get ready, Carol bought new shoes for $36.00 and a new water bottle for $1.36. Her mom gave her $47.00 to spend.

   a. How much did she spend for the shoes and water bottle?

   _____

   b. How much more were the shoes than the water bottle? _____

Who's Who?

Mr. Fitzpatrick has three boys in his class who go by variations of the name Robert. From the statements below, determine each boy's full name and age. Mark an "**O**" in each correct box and an "**X**" in the boxes that are not correct.

1. Wilson is younger than Robert but older than Johnson.

2. Bobby is not the youngest.

3. None of the boys are the same age.

4. Anderson is the oldest.

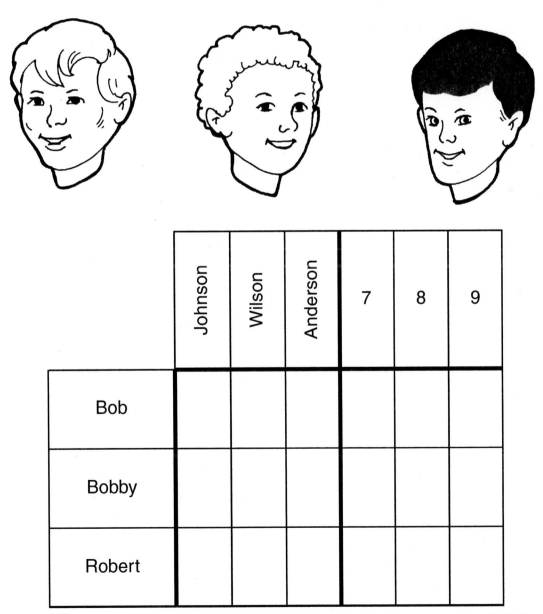

	Johnson	Wilson	Anderson	7	8	9
Bob						
Bobby						
Robert						

Change for Fifty Cents

There are over 75 ways to make change for 50 cents. Work with a friend to list as many ways as you can. List the coins in order on each line, from largest to smallest. (*Hint:* Working from large to small coins will also help you find more ways to make change.) The list has been started for you.

Use the following abbreviations:

hd (half dollar)   q (quarter)   d (dime)   n (nickel)   p (penny)

1. 1 hd

2. 2 q

3. _____

4. _____

5. _____

6. _____

7. _____

8. _____

9. _____

10. _____

11. _____

12. _____

13. _____

14. _____

15. _____

16. _____

17. _____

18. _____

19. _____

20. _____

More Who's Who?

Mr. Martin has three boys in his science class who each go by a variation of the name Theodore. From the statements below, discover each boy's full name and age. Mark the correct boxes with an "**O**" and the incorrect boxes with an "**X**".

1. Agee is younger than Dalton but older than Chin.

2. Ted is not the youngest or the oldest.

3. Theodore's last name is Chin.

4. None of the boys are the same age.

	Agee	Chin	Dalton	8	9	10
Ted						
Theodore						
Teddy						

Shapes

The four shapes shown below are:

_____　　　_____

_____　　　_____

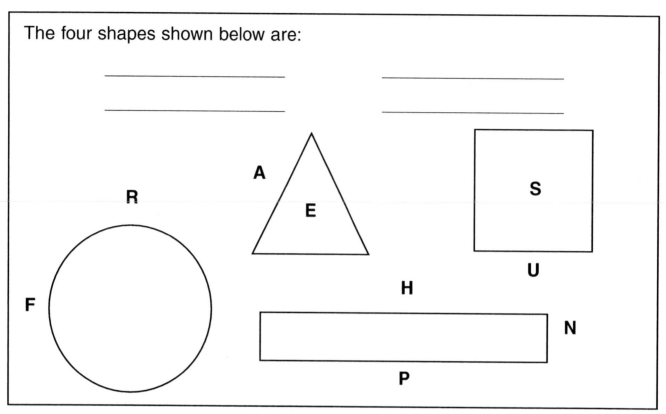

Directions: Answer the questions in the correct box to discover the hidden message.

Write the letter to the right of the rectangle in box 12.

Write the letter to the left of the triangle in boxes 3 and 7.

Write the letter under the rectangle in box 4.

Write the letter above the rectangle in box 2.

Write the letter inside the triangle in boxes 5 and 9.

Write the letter under the square in box 11.

Write the letter inside the square in boxes 1 and 6.

Write the letter above the circle in box 8.

Write the letter to the left of the circle in box 10.

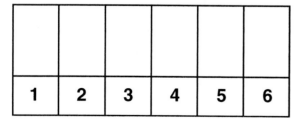

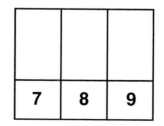

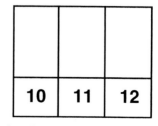

Escape the Volcano

Complete each math problem. Eight answers have the number 4 in them; they show the only safe way across the island to avoid the lava. Draw a line to show the way across.

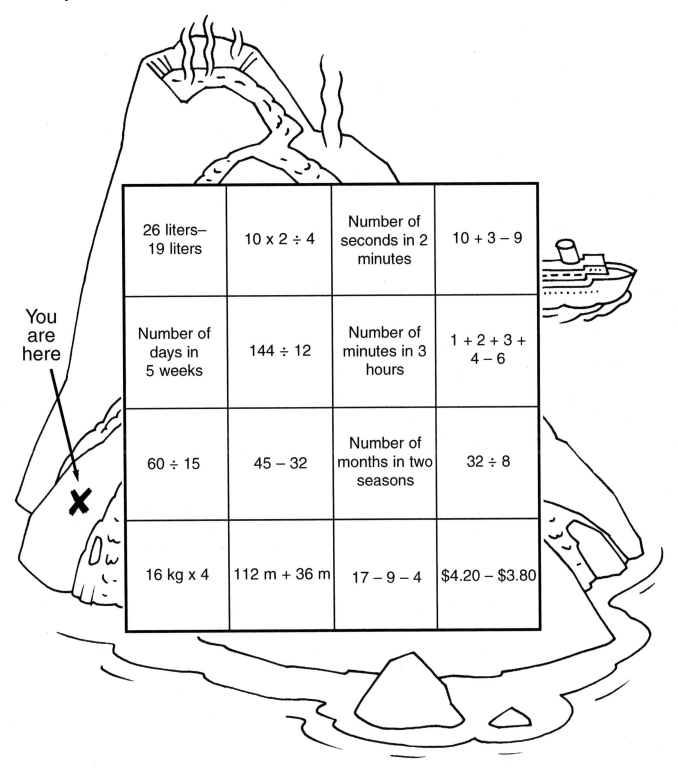

You
are
here

26 liters– 19 liters	10 x 2 ÷ 4	Number of seconds in 2 minutes	10 + 3 – 9
Number of days in 5 weeks	144 ÷ 12	Number of minutes in 3 hours	1 + 2 + 3 + 4 – 6
60 ÷ 15	45 – 32	Number of months in two seasons	32 ÷ 8
16 kg x 4	112 m + 36 m	17 – 9 – 4	$4.20 – $3.80

Math Puzzles

1. Two jugs are marked 5 L and 3 L. Show how they can be used to measure exactly 7 liters of water.

2. Until last week, all the dogs at Bob's Kennels (pictured below) had their own enclosures. Three more dogs will arrive this week. What is the fewest number of new walls Bob will have to build to make sure each dog will have its own enclosure?

3. A new clock has been invented which looks like this:

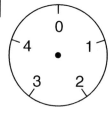

- 2 + 2 means start at 2 and move clockwise 2 numbers. (2 + 2 = 4)

- 0 − 1 means start at 0 and move counter-clockwise 1 number. (0 − 1 = 4)

- 4 x 2 means start at 0 and make 4 moves of 2 numbers clockwise.
  (4 x 2 = 3)

What times are represented here?

1 + 2 = _____	1 x 3 = _____	3 + 3 = _____
3 x 2 = _____	4 − 3 = _____	2 − 3 = _____

Alphabet Animals

Find names of animals for each letter of the alphabet. Write as many as you can think of for each letter. For example, for the letter "**D**" you could write: dog, duck, dinosaur, deer, etc.

A _____

B _____

C _____

D _____

E _____

F _____

G _____

H _____

I _____

J _____

K _____

L _____

M _____

Alphabet Animals *(cont.)*

N _____

O _____

P _____

Q _____

R _____

S _____

T _____

U _____

V _____

W _____

X _____

Y _____

Z _____

Alphabet Shapes

Print the alphabet using capital letters in three groups of shapes.

letters with all straight lines

letters with all curved lines

letters with both straight and curved lines

Treasure Island Word Hunt

There are lots of words in the book *Treasure Island*—and there are lots of words hidden in the words "Treasure Island," too. Because there are so many, we're making it easier for you—you only have to find five-letter words—and they can't be plurals ending in "S." List all the words you find.

TREASURE ISLAND

Riddle

Riddle: What do dentists in court trials have to swear?

1. Assemble the three-letter groups into one long line following the order of the spiral (starting from DYU).

2. Add 12 letter "O"s.

3. Answer the riddle!

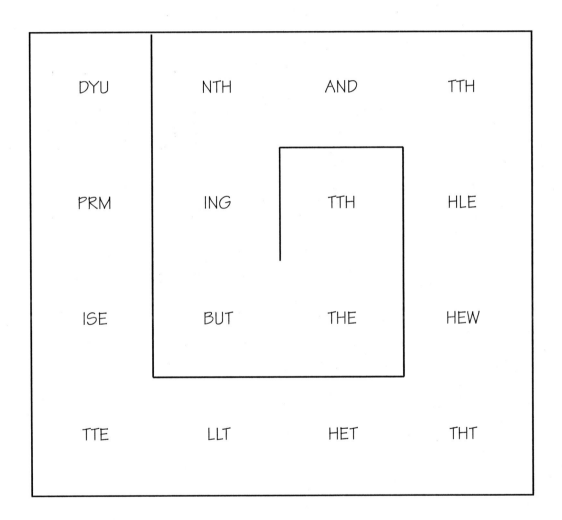

And the answer is . . . _____

Sally in Space

It took Sally a long time to get into space. How long will it take you to change STARS into SPACE? Use each clue to form a new word, but you can only change one letter at a time.

S	T	A	R	S	
					fights
					extra
S	P	A	C	E	

What's in a Word: Napoleon

How many four (or more) letter words can you make from the word *Napoleon*?

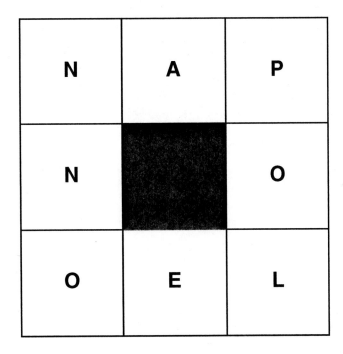

Keeping a Tab on Things

Steph is learning how to play the guitar using tablature, a music reading system where numbers are used to represent the notes on the different strings. After playing a few tunes, she discovered she could make words from the different notes. Can you discover what each word is?

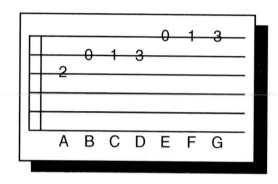

1.

_____

2.

_____

3.

_____

4.

_____

Spic-and-Span Spinach

Spinach the vegetable—full of vitamins and minerals! Spinach the word—full of other words! How many three- (or more) letter words can you find in spinach? You may not use plurals. (*Hint:* There are two words in the title!)

SPINACH

Alliteration Challenge

Peter Pan's name is alliterative; it has the same consonant (P) at the beginning of each word. Can you match up these other alliterative characters?

Black	**Tucker**
Doctor	**Duck**
Donald	**Doolittle**
Goosey	**Beauty**
Maid	**Mouse**
Mickey	**Rabbit**
Miss	**Marion**
Mister	**Gander**
Peter	**McGregor**
Roger	**Pan**
Tommy	**Muffet**

Weather Report

The weather forecast is in. But the words (which should be in the middle row of each grid) are missing. Find them by completing each of the three-letter words going down the grid.

C	S	B	A
Y	D	D	Y

S	P	W	O
E	T	T	D

A	I	P	S	O
E	L	T	M	D

O	H	A
F	G	E

Secret Code

Crack the code to figure out the message.

A	B	C	D	E	F	G	H	I	J	K	L	M
○	□	♥	✳	▲	❄	◇	→	☆	✪	⇨	♣	▼

N	O	P	Q	R	S	T	U	V	W	X	Y	Z
🐦	☞	✂	✈	❖	◗	■	✐	✍	✚	☆	⊛	❀

❖ ▲ ○ ✳ ☆ 🐦 ◇

☆ ◗   ♣ ☞ ■ ◗   ☞ ❄

❄ ✐ 🐦 !

Rhyming Word Pairs

Find two words that rhyme and have about the same meaning as the phrase that is given. An example has been done for you.

bashful insect = shy fly

1. chicken yard _____

2. distant sun _____

3. warm pan _____

4. rabbit stool _____

5. boat journey _____

6. runaway fowl _____

7. good sleep _____

8. angry father _____

9. large fake hair _____

10. reading area _____

11. not fast bird _____

12. a group of noon eaters _____

13. damp plane _____

14. sweet rodents _____

15. kitty cap _____

Three-Letter Words

Each of the following words has a synonym that contains three letters. Write them on the lines.

1. work   ___ ___ ___

2. crazy   ___ ___ ___

3. fresh   ___ ___ ___

4. ancient   ___ ___ ___

5. sick   ___ ___ ___

6. every   ___ ___ ___

7. auto   ___ ___ ___

8. repair   ___ ___ ___

9. consume   ___ ___ ___

10. plump   ___ ___ ___

11. finish   ___ ___ ___

12. lad   ___ ___ ___

13. feline   ___ ___ ___

14. remark   ___ ___ ___

15. attempt   ___ ___ ___

Rhyming Word Pairs

Find an adjective that rhymes with a noun so that together the two words have about the same meaning as the phrase that is given. An example has been done for you.

soaked dog = soggy doggy

1. heavy slumber   _____

2. second male sibling   _____

3. able Daniel   _____

4. big flat boat   _____

5. naked bunny   _____

6. high shopping center   _____

7. crazy kid   _____

8. wooden lower limb   _____

9. igloo   _____

10. tuna dinner   _____

11. consume beef   _____

12. funny William   _____

13. heavy feline   _____

14. impolite man   _____

15. extra bus money   _____

16. short cry   _____

17. extra points   _____

18. aging green stuff   _____

19. downcast father   _____

20. loafing flower   _____

What Can You Make from Celluloid?

Celluloid was used for manufacturing a huge variety of items. Can you manufacture a huge variety of words? List all the words you can find using the letters in celluloid.

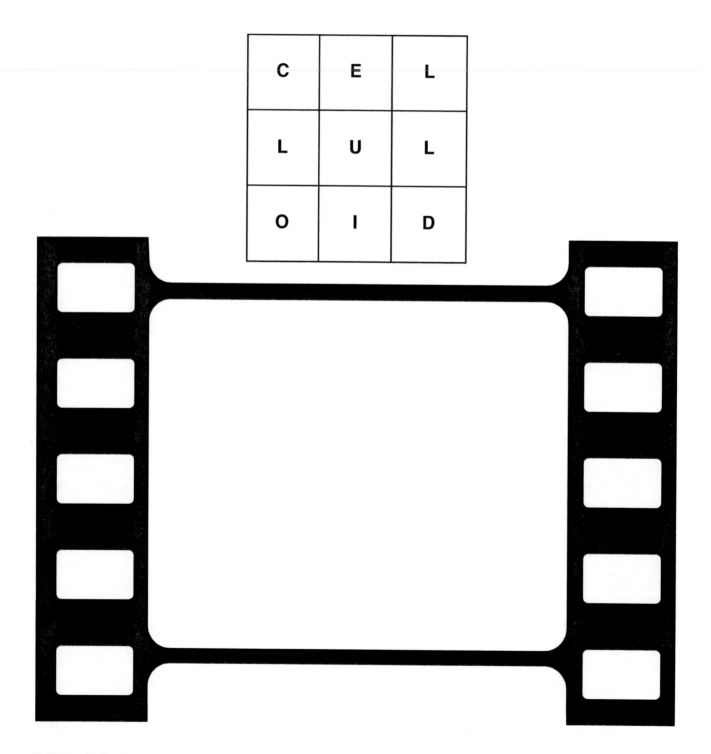

C	E	L
L	U	L
O	I	D

Only in America...

How many words of three letters or more can you make from the word AMERICA?

What Could It Be?

1. List some things that are smaller than your hand. Draw some of the items from your list in the box on the right.

2. What can be hidden under your shoe? Draw some of the items from your list in the box on the right.

3. What can you balance on your hand? Draw some the items from your list in the box on the right.

The Trancapar

Draw a trancapar. (There is no such thing as a trancapar, so it can be anything you like.)

Write a story of what happened to the trancapar last Tuesday.

_____

_____

_____

_____

_____

_____

What a Tale!

Write a story about the toaster and the cat. You can add other things to your story as you write it.

Any Animal

If you could be any animal in the world, which animal would you choose? Give at least five reasons for your choice. Draw a picture of your animal.

The Circus #1

Write a story about "My First Circus" from the point of view of a clown who is performing in one of the acts.

_____

_____

_____

_____

_____

_____

_____

_____

_____

_____

_____

_____

The Circus #2

Start a story with this beginning: It was my first visit to the circus. I was very excited. Suddenly, the crowd went quiet. I looked up and could not believe my eyes. . .

You Won!

You have just won $50. You have to spend it all on your dog. Describe how you would spend your money.

Imagine . . .

Imagine you are only 6 inches (15 centimeters) tall. How would the world be different?

_____

_____

_____

_____

_____

_____

_____

_____

_____

_____

_____

_____

Promoting Your Least Favorite Subject

Be a copywriter and write a radio commercial for your least favorite school subject. (That's hard since you don't like the subject, but hey, advertising agencies have to do it all the time!)

Magic and Make-believe

What if Cinderella's Fairy Godmother could perform some magic for the Three Little Pigs and the Big Bad Wolf? What do you think they would ask for?

_____

_____

_____

_____

_____

_____

_____

_____

_____

_____

_____

Life in a Goldfish Bowl

Pretend you are a goldfish. Think of a name for yourself and fill in the information below.

My name is _____.

I am a_____.

I eat _____.

Good things about living in a goldfish bowl.

Bad things about living in a goldfish bowl.

One day something terrible happened to me . . .

Clever Categories

Create categories for the following words and then divide the words into those groups. Put the words into their categories in the space below.

girl	chair	sock
butter	unicorn	egg
castle	cat	tree
apple	fairy	waterfall
forest	train	bicycle
cake	frog	fire engine

How Could You . . . ?

List all the different ways you could travel to school tomorrow:

_____

_____

_____

_____

_____

List how you could make people laugh:

_____

_____

_____

_____

List other ways to use a magazine besides reading it:

_____

_____

_____

_____

List different uses for a spoonful of peanut butter:

_____

_____

_____

_____

More How Could You . . . ?

Think of ways that you could

. . . brush your hair without a hairbrush or comb.

. . . write a story without pencil or paper.

. . . get dressed without using clothes.

What If?

What if your friends all grew three feet taller in one night?

What if it rained milk?

What if people were born old and became younger?

Make a Picture

Choose a shape and change it into . . .

a car	a house	an imaginary friend	a dog

Jack and the Beanstalk

Imagine that Jack is climbing up the beanstalk. Draw four different pictures of what he might have seen as he climbed higher and higher.

Change the Chair

Redesign the chair using the BAR system. Explain your reasons for making the changes.

B = make it Bigger or smaller

A = Add something

R = Remove something and Replace it with something else

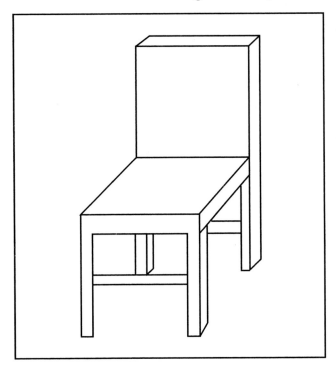

B

Reasons _____

_____

A

Reasons _____

_____

R

Reasons _____

_____

What Are These?

1. If they are eyes, what is 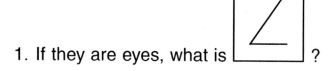 ?   _____

2. If they are heads, what are 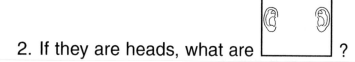 ?   _____

3. If they are balls, what is 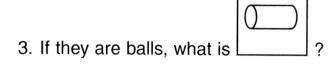 ?   _____

4. If they are hoops, what is 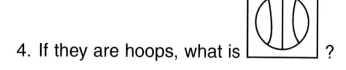 ?   _____

5. If they are earrings, what is 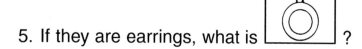 ?   _____

6. If they are round windows, what is  ?   _____

7. If they are holes in the road, what is 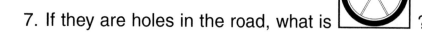 ?   _____

8. If they are oranges, what is 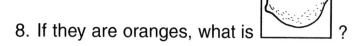 ?   _____

What is the Same?
What is Different?

Use the acronym SCUMPS to compare the two objects. List everything that you can think of about the objects that is the same or different.

S = Size   Same: _____

                  Different: _____

C = Color   Same: _____

                  Different: _____

U = Use   Same: _____

                  Different: _____

M = Materials   Same: _____

                  Different: _____

P = Parts   Same: _____

                  Different: _____

S = Shape   Same: _____

                  Different: _____

What Are These Splotches?

This is a baby bird with its beak open. It is crying for food.
Write in the space what each splotch could be.

_____

_____

_____

_____

_____

_____

_____

_____

_____

_____

_____

_____

_____

_____

_____

The Future

Design new tools and vehicles that community helpers (examples: firefighters, policemen, nurses might be able to use in the future.

Draw diagrams of your inventions with labels for their parts. Explain how your inventions would work.

_____

_____

_____

_____

People Who Help in the Community

1. Draw some of the equipment these community helpers use.

Fire Fighters	Police Officers	Ambulance Drivers

2. Draw an emergency where all three of the above community helpers have been called upon to work together.

3. Describe what happened.

_____

_____

_____

_____

A Different School

Design a new school. You can decide what the school will be called and what type of lessons are to be taught.

My new school will be called _____.

This is what my new school will look like.	
Lessons to be taught	**When**

I would like these lessons because _____

_____

_____

_____

Three important school rules will be:

1. _____

2. _____

3. _____

A New Toy

Develop a new toy that has wheels, wings, feet, and springs.

In the spaces below, write how many of each item your toy will have and draw what each part will look like.

Wheels	Wings	Feet	Springs

My toy will be called: _____

This is what my toy can do: _____

_____

_____

Draw how you and your friends could use this toy.

The best thing about this toy is: _____

_____

Famous Sports People

1. Draw a picture of a famous sports person. Write some facts about this person.

   Name: _____

   Sport: _____

   Sport equipment used:

   _____

   _____

2. If you were to meet this person, what two questions would you like to ask him or her?

   a. _____

   b. _____

3. List four skills you would need to be good at this sport.

   Draw pictures of yourself practicing these skills.

Skill:	Skill:
Skill:	**Skill:**

Food

1. Draw a picture of each food.

| apple | potato | carrot | banana | orange |

| cake | sausages | ice cream | tomato | biscuits |

2. Sort these foods into different groups. For example, an apple is a healthy food.

Healthy Food	Unhealthy Food

Eating

Which of these foods would you like to eat for lunch?

Answer **Yes** or **No**

1. a cheese sandwich _____

2. a bucket of nails _____

3. leaves _____

4. an apple _____

5. yogurt _____

6. snail sausages _____

7. grapes _____

8. a chocolate worm _____

9. a banana _____

10. spider jelly _____

Imagine that you can eat anything you want for breakfast. List the items below and then draw a picture of what you would eat.

I would eat the following items:

1. _____   2. _____   3. _____

Environment Watch

1. What kind of damage has been done to the environment by modern methods of transportation?

_____

_____

_____

_____

_____

2. Draw a picture of some of the damage that has been caused by the various types of transportation.

```



```

3. Can anything be done to improve this, or is it too late?

Write your thoughts here: _____

_____

_____

_____

School Travel

Invent a new way you could travel to school. Draw a picture of your invented vehicle.

Patch the Balloon

The Montgolfier brothers' balloon was made up of two different colored stripes. Soon it got a few holes in it and had to be patched. The brothers didn't want any patch to touch a stripe of the same color, or another patch of the same color. What is the least number of colors they could use?

Taxi Ride

You've been lecturing on transportation systems at the city museum but it's time to return home. So, you call for a taxi.

1. Turn left onto East Terrace.

2. Take the second right.

3. Take the next right and then left.

4. Turn at the next right and pick up a passenger.

5. Turn right, cross the intersection, and stop. Pick up more passengers.

6. Turn right, then left.

7. Turn right, then right again. Cross the next intersection and stop. Get out of the taxi and leave town.

Questions:

1. How many people are in the taxi altogether? _____

2. How did you leave town? _____

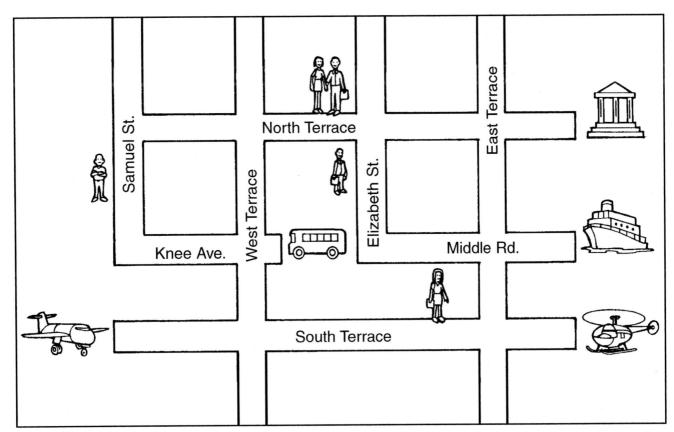

Stamp Forgery

List as many differences as you can find between the original stamp and the fake stamp below.

Original

Fake

_____

_____

_____

_____

_____

_____

_____

_____

_____

Postcard Rebus

Your lucky friend is on a round-the-world trip. You've received lots of postcards but sometimes it's tricky finding out just where in the world they've come from. Can you decode these countries' names?

1. _____	NEW + + P̸ Z 2. _____	IT 3. _____
👁 + 4. _____	+ I̶E̶S̶ 5. _____	+ S 6. _____
+ ADA 7. _____	IS + 8. _____	PURR + OO 9. _____

Spot the Difference

Two landscape artists drew the same landscape, but on different days and at different times. Can you spot the ten differences?

A Light Humor

Match up the joke and the correct answer for a chuckle. Match up the joke and the incorrect answer for a real laugh.

Joke	Answer

| 1. Why was the lighthouse keeper fired? | a nervous wreck |

| 2. Why did the overweight captain change jobs? | and cargoes go in ships? |

| 3. How do you know the sea is friendly? | Both crews were marooned. |

| 4. Did you hear about the red ship and the blue ship that collided? | He couldn't sleep with the light on. |

| 5. Why do shipments go in cars? | It's always waving. |

| 6. Why did the lighthouse keeper go crazy? | The spiral staircase drove him around the bend. |

| 7. How can you tell lighthouses are happy? | They beam all the time. |

| 8. What lies on the bottom of the ocean and shivers? | to become a light housekeeper |

The Limbo of the Lost Yachts!

The Bermuda Triangle strikes again, snaring five yachts in its mysterious maze-like currents. Fortunately, four of the yachts can escape.

Which is the unlucky one? _____

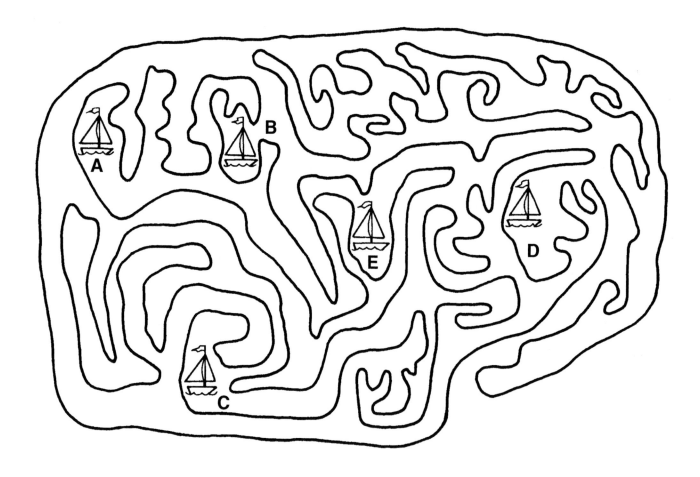

Plastic Memory Game

Look carefully at the picture below. It shows 12 different objects. Each object is made completely out of plastic or plastic parts. Looked long enough? On the following page, write a list of as many items as you can remember.

Plastic Memory Game *(cont.)*

How many objects can you remember? List them below.

_____

_____

_____

_____

_____

_____

_____

_____

_____

_____

_____

In My School Room

Draw a picture of a school room with the following items in it.

1 chalkboard   1 picture   4 books   3 chairs   3 tables

Equations

Each equation below contains the initials of words that will make it complete.
Find the missing words. An example has been done for you.

9 P in the S S = 9 Planets in the Solar System

1. 26 L in the A = _____

2. 52 C in a D = _____

3. 88 P K = _____

4. 3 B M (S H T R) = _____

5. 4 Q in a G = _____

6. 11 P on a F T = _____

7. 7 C on the E = _____

8. 50 S in the U S = _____

9. 6 P for a T = _____

10. 20,000 L U the S = _____

11. 1,001 A N = _____

12. 5 D in a Z C = _____

13. 5 F on the R or L H = _____

14. 4 S in the Y = _____

15. 8 S on a S S = _____

School of the future

Design a school of the future that would really appeal to children. Sketch and label some of your ideas below.

Elephant Jokes

Match these elephant jokes to the funniest answer.

Questions

| How do you get an elephant out of the water? |
| What do you call any elephant that is an expert on skin disorders? |
| What has two tails, two trunks, and five feet? |
| What is beautiful, gray, and wears very big glass slippers? |
| What's gray on the inside and pink and white on the outside? |
| What's gray, yellow, gray, yellow . . .? |
| Why do elephants wear sandals? |
| Why are elephants wrinkled? |
| How do you stop an elephant from charging? |

Answers

| A pachydermatologist |
| An elephant rolling down a hill with a daisy in its mouth |
| An elephant with spare parts |
| An inside-out elephant |
| Take away its credit card |
| Cinderelephant |
| Have you ever tried to iron one? |
| So that they don't sink in the sand |
| wet |

What a Racket!

1. Glasses

2. Make lenses bigger so frames don't interfere with vision.

3. Add sunshades, so sun doesn't get in the eyes.

4. Replace earpieces with elastic, so glasses stay on when playing sports.

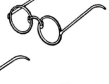

Design a new and improved tennis racket using **BAR** to help you. Draw and explain each change. 	**B** Make it **B**igger.
A **A**dd something.	**R** **R**eplace, change or **R**earrange.

Fairy Tale Designer

Design a business card for the Big Bad Wolf.

Create a different outfit for Little Red Riding Hood.

Crazy Combinations

Brainstorm a list of different fruit and follow this with a list of different animals. Draw an **anifruit** by combining features of one of the animals and one of the fruits. Give your **anifruit** a name. For example, a combination of an apricot and a cat could be an apricat or invent any name that feels appropriate. Describe what your anifruit does, what it likes, and what it doesn't like.

What Can it Be?

A.

B.
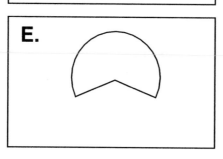

C.

D.

E.

F.
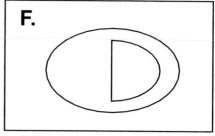

Look at the pictures and write what you think they could be. You can look at them in any way—sideways, backwards, right side up, or upside-down.

It's something to do with school. What is it?	It's something to do with the holidays. What is it?
A _____	A _____
B _____	B _____
C _____	C _____
D _____	D _____
E _____	E _____
F _____	F _____

An Ideal Pet

Create an animal that can fly, swim, walk, climb, carry you for long distances, and would make an ideal pet. Draw a picture of your pet and tell about it.

_____

_____

_____

_____

_____

Brain Workouts

Multiplication and Division Word Problems

Read each problem and then answer the questions.

The Bailey family runs a small market that not only sells but also grows fresh fruit and vegetables. They sell gardening tools, seeds, and plants. They help their customers with questions about picking which plants to grow and how to best care for them.

1. Two hundred fifteen watermelon seeds were planted in the ground. Five seeds were planted in each small hole. How many small holes were there?

2. The gardeners at Bailey's Market planted 48 onions in each of 12 rows. How many onions were planted?

3. A clerk sold Garrett a rake for $7.75 and a shovel for $13.77. He paid half and had his brother pay the other half. How much did each pay?

Multiplication and Division
Word Problems *(cont.)*

Read each problem and then answer the questions.

4. Tim bought 2,000 carrot seeds on Monday and 3,985 seeds on Tuesday. He needs to plant all of the seeds. He plants seven seeds in each hole. How many holes will he have when he is finished?

5. Randy planted seven rows of corn and each row had eight plants in it. He needed to wrap them into bundles of four. How many bundles would he have?

6. Two customers each bought 25 potatoes for a pot luck supper. They made 10 pots of stew and used all of the potatoes. How many potatoes did they use in each stew?

Multiplication and Division
Word Problems *(cont.)*

Read each problem and then answer the questions.

7. Each seed packet costs $.79. R____n bought nine of them. How much did she spend?

8. Each _____ Robyn will need to plant 15 seeds in a row.

9. What wil_____ rapes at $2.00 each, one bag of potatoes _____ f strawberries at $3.46 each?

10. The worker _____ at has the apples in it.
    There are s_____ s.
    Each bin ha_____ pples are
    there in the ____

Change These Shapes

Create interesting objects from these shapes. Under each drawing explain what you have drawn.

My Perfect Day

Write out a timetable for your perfect day.

For example: 8:00 A.M.—wake up and eat *ice cream* for breakfast.

Time	Event
_____	_____
_____	_____
_____	_____
_____	_____
_____	_____
_____	_____
_____	_____
_____	_____
_____	_____
_____	_____
_____	_____

What's the Question?

The answer is 50. What are 15 questions?

1. _____

2. _____

3. _____

4. _____

5. _____

6. _____

7. _____

8. _____

9. _____

10. _____

11. _____

12. _____

13. _____

14. _____

15. _____

Audition for Trivia Show

You have been asked to audition for a television quiz show called *Number Trivia.*
The television producer asks you to solve the following problem:

- Circle sets of three numbers that add up to eight.

- You can only circle each number once.

- When circling numbers you may not cross another line.

- You must use all of the numbers.

2	0	8	0	1
1	5	4	7	0
3	1	3	5	1
4	1	1	5	2
7	0	0	2	0
1	8	0	7	1

Audition for Trivia Show *(cont.)*

Imagine you have been hired as assistant television producer. Design a problem similar to the previous problem for another contestant to solve.

Measurement Mysteries

Solve this mystery.

a. Fred sells flour and potatoes in the market. In this market, a bucket filled with sand—a "sacket"—is the accepted measure of weight. Fred sells his flour for $1.79 per sacket and his potatoes for $2.47 per sacket. Frieda is a customer who buys seven sackets of flour and three sackets of potatoes. How much change will she receive if she pays with a $20 bill?

b. After receiving her change, Frieda finds a $5 bill in her purse. She doesn't like change and wants to spend as much of this money as she can. What can she buy from Fred that will leave her with the least amount of change?

A New Jail

The Police Commissioner of Toothpick City designed a brand new jail with 13 toothpicks. This jail had six cells for the prisoners. When he showed the design to the mayor, the mayor said he didn't like the shape. The mayor said, "If you used 12 toothpicks instead, you could have a much more interesting looking jail with the same number of cells."

Task: Use 12 toothpicks to build the new jail.

Old Jail

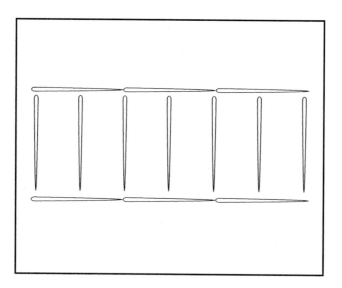

New Jail

A New Jail *(cont.)*

Now try these!

1 Start with 12 toothpicks in square 1.

2. In square 2 move two toothpicks and make 2 squares.

3. In square 3 move three toothpicks and leave only 3 squares.

1.

2.

3.

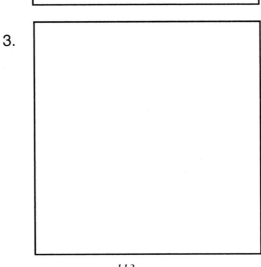

Speeding Along

To calculate the average speed of a moving object, divide the distance traveled by the time taken. For example, a car travels 44 km in two hours. Its average speed is 44 ÷ 2 km/hour, i.e. 22 km/hour

Calculate the average speed of each of these moving objects.

1. A plane travels 1,470 km in three hours.   _____

2. A snail travels 55 cm in 11 minutes.   _____

3. A cyclist travels 95 km in five hours.   _____

4. A racing car travels 320 km in two hours.   _____

5. A dad with a baby carriage travels 2,000 m in 40 minutes.   _____

6. The space shuttle travels five km in 10 hours. (Careful!)   _____

   Why did the space shuttle travel so slowly?   _____

   _____

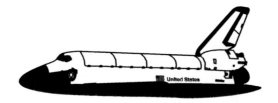

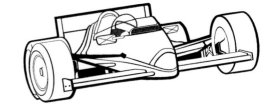

Recording Time Line

The past 100 years has seen sound recording progress from the wax cylinders of Edison's original phonograph through to the DVDs being installed in many computers. Use the clues to place all these recording inventions on the circular time line.

Cassette: Invented just in time to record the Beatles.

CD: Wow! They're about 20 years old!

DAT: Digital Audio Tape. Mainly found in videos, invented 93 years after the phonograph.

DVD: The latest and greatest!

Gramophone: The first flat record.

LP: Long-playing record. Invented 50 years after the tape recorder.

Phonograph: The first sound recording device.

Tape recorder: Invented in the 19th century.

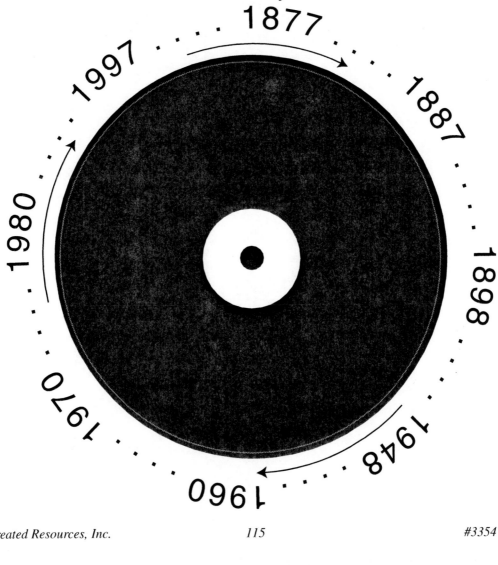

Island Math

The navigator on the Santa Maria has an unusual way of recording the year in which the expedition lands on each island. Can you figure out which were discovered in the same year as Columbus set sail?

373 x 4

186 x 8

1492 x 1

165 x 9

213 x 7

298 x 5

248 x 6

497 x 3

746 x 2

I've Been Framed!

Each number in the boxes below is written within a different shape or frame. Using this as a guide, write the correct number in each shape below and solve each problem.

8	3	5
6	9	7
4	2	1

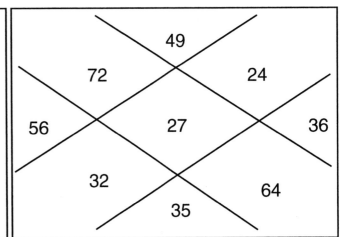

1. $(\wedge \div \llcorner) \times (\lozenge \div \sqcup) = \underline{\quad}$

2. $(\diagup\rangle \div \urcorner) \times (\vee \div \square) = \underline{\quad}$

3. $(\vee\rangle \div \square) \times (\langle \div \lrcorner) = \underline{\quad}$

4. $(\rangle \div \square) \times (\ulcorner \div \lrcorner) = \underline{\quad}$

5. $(\langle \div \daleth) \times (\wedge \div \square) = \underline{\quad}$

At the Zoo

Melanie, Jessica, Sarah, and Rachael went to the zoo last Saturday. Each girl saw her favorite animal and ate her favorite food. From the clues given, determine each girl's favorite animal and food. (*Hint:* No two girls have the same favorite food or animal.)

1. Melanie loves the wolves but does not like lollipops or chocolate bars.

2. Sarah is afraid of the jaguars.

3. The girl who loves jaguars does not eat chocolate bars or potato chips, but the girl who eats hot dogs loves the gorillas.

4. Jessica enjoys any kind of chocolate bar.

	Jaguars	Wolves	Gorillas	Ponies	Chocolate bars	Lollipops	Potato chips	Hot dogs
Melanie								
Sarah								
Rachael								
Jessica								

Number System

Invent a new number system. Write five problems and answers using any new symbols.

Example: ▲ + ★ = ☉

1. _____

2. _____

3. _____

4. _____

5. _____

The Decimal Fraction Derby

And they're off! There's No Chance in the outside lane, Fat Chance in the middle lane, and Slim Chance in the inside lane. Who will win the derby? Add each number each horse crosses—the horse with the lowest total at the end wins!

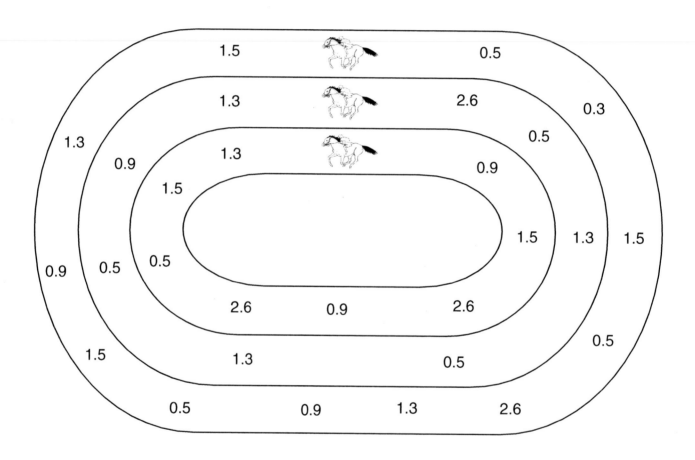

Final Count

No Chance _____

Fat Chance _____

Slim Chance _____

Lucky Three-Leaf Clovers

What a shame! All these leaves and not one of them a lucky four-leaf clover.
Ah, but ONE of them is lucky; three times luckier than all the others! Can you
figure out which one it is?

Mail Muddle-up

Andre, Ben, Cindy, and Daphne's mail is in the mailbox. There is a parcel, a postcard, a bill, and a letter (not necessarily in order). They have been sent by a mom, a dad, a baker, and an aunt (also not necessarily in order). Three items have stamps: flowers, pets, and a building. One item has no stamp. Use the information below to discover who got what from which sender and with what stamp.

1. Andre's mail was not a postcard, didn't come from his mom, and had no stamp.

2. Cindy passed on the parcel with the flower stamp to the correct person.

3. One person was jealous because they only got a postcard, while her sister got a parcel.

4. The dad put the wrong child's name on his mail.

5. One person's mail, sender, and stamp were alliterative with that person's name!

Birthday Cake

Can you cut a birthday cake into eight pieces, using only three cuts?

Show how you would do this.

Who Won the Race?

Seven snails competed in the inaugural Compost Heap to the Vegetable Garden Race. Use the information below to learn who came in where:

1. Edward finished before Francis, but after Denise.

2. Bernard could only see Abigail in front of him at the finish.

3. Gabby got fed up seeing Francis' shell for the whole race.

4. Cathryn finished before Denise.

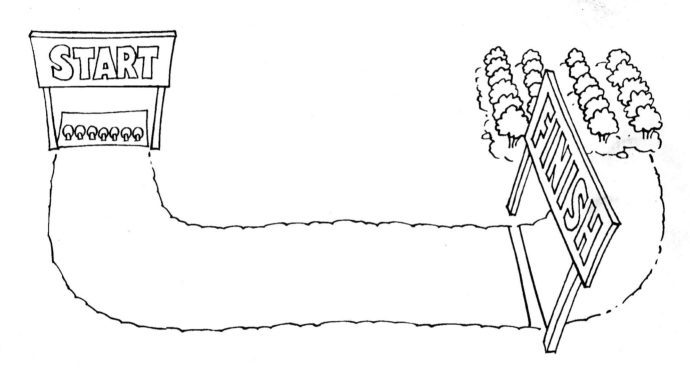

Draw a picture of the seven snails, showing who won, and what place the other snails finished. Explain how you solved the problem.

_____

_____

_____

Spot the Water Bird

Water birds are often well camouflaged to protect them from predators and there are ten well-hidden in the words below. To find them, complete these word problems by 'subtracting' letters from the main word or words and unscrambling the remaining letters.

1. SUN DECK – ENS = _____

2. GENUINE PART – TARE = _____

3. APPLIANCE – AP = _____

4. NEWS CAST – TECS = _____

5. GLUE BOTTLE – EETTBO = _____

6. LOOKS GREAT– RATLK = _____

7. LONG BOOK – OKBG = _____

8. FRANCE – F = _____

9. REGRET – R = _____

10. STRIPED PANTS – TST = _____

What's in the Bag? #1

Read the words on the next page. Then match the letters with the correct synonyms in the clues. (You will not use all of the letters.) Put the five clues together and discover what's in the bag!

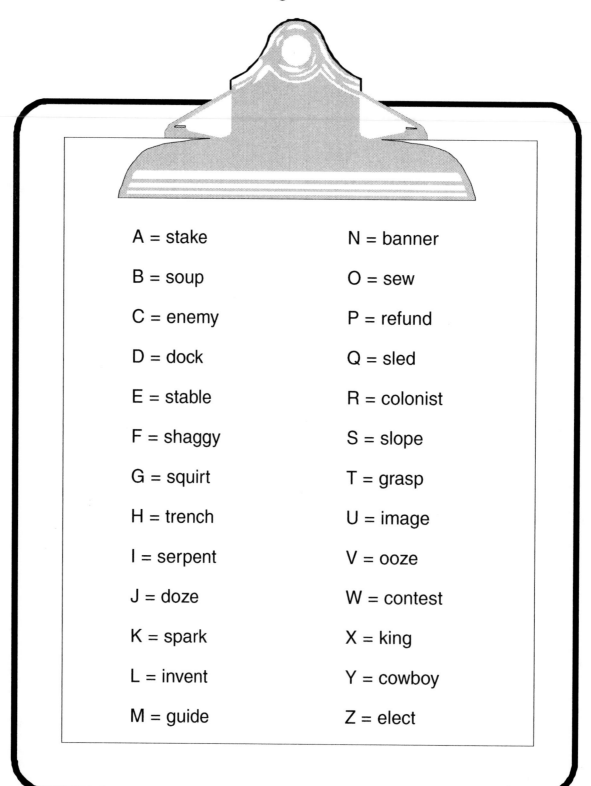

A = stake

B = soup

C = enemy

D = dock

E = stable

F = shaggy

G = squirt

H = trench

I = serpent

J = doze

K = spark

L = invent

M = guide

N = banner

O = sew

P = refund

Q = sled

R = colonist

S = slope

T = grasp

U = image

V = ooze

W = contest

X = king

Y = cowboy

Z = elect

What's in the Bag? #1 (cont.)

Clue 1:

____ ____ ____ ____ ____
slant seize barn barn create

Clue 2:

____ ____ ____ ____ ____
slant ditch post settler repay

Clue 3:

____ ____ ____ ____ ____
nap stitch snake flag slant

Clue 4:

____ ____ ____ ____
race stitch stitch pier

Clue 5:

____ ____ ____ ____ ____ ____
ditch post leader leader barn settler

What's in the bag? _____

What's in the Bag? #2

Read the words on the next page. Then match the letters with the correct synonyms in the clues. (You will not use all of the letters.) Put the five clues together and discover what's in the bag!

A = anger

B = purchase

C = sorcerer

D = timid

E = calm

F = grief

G = rule

H = canine

I = feline

J = ache

K = misty

L = dense

M = sincere

N = late

O = peppy

P = mix

Q = thump

R = lanky

S = lather

T = grass

U = riddle

V = nation

W = power

Y = grease

Z = wind

What's in the Bag? #2 (cont.)

Clue 1:

_____   _____   _____   _____   _____   _____

suds   witch   rage   thick   quiet   suds

Clue 2:

_____   _____   _____   _____   _____   _____   _____

suds   thick   cat   lawn   dog   quiet   tall

Clue 3:

_____   _____   _____   _____   _____

witch   spry   cat   thick   suds

Clue 4:

_____   _____   _____   _____

thick   spry   tardy   govern

Clue 5:

_____   _____   _____   _____

honest   spry   thick   lawn

What's in the bag? _____

What's in the Bag? #3

Read the words on the next page. Then match the letters with the correct synonyms in the clues. (You will not use all the letters.) Put the five clues together and discover what's in the bag!

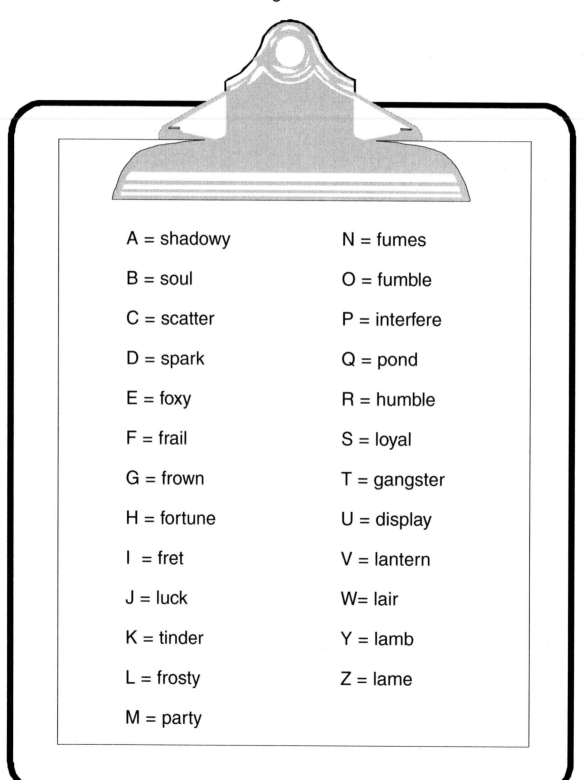

A = shadowy

B = soul

C = scatter

D = spark

E = foxy

F = frail

G = frown

H = fortune

I = fret

J = luck

K = tinder

L = frosty

M = party

N = fumes

O = fumble

P = interfere

Q = pond

R = humble

S = loyal

T = gangster

U = display

V = lantern

W = lair

Y = lamb

Z = lame

What's in the Bag? #3 (cont.)

Clue 1:

_____ _____ _____ _____ _____ _____ _____

faithful   outlaw   poor   dark   gases   scowl   crafty

Clue 2:

_____ _____ _____ _____ _____ _____ _____ _____ _____

faithful meddle dark disperse crafty faithful riches worry meddle

Clue 3:

_____ _____ _____ _____ _____ _____

riches   mistake   lamp   crafty   poor   faithful

Clue 4:

_____ _____ _____ _____ _____ _____

dark   freezing   worry   crafty   gases   faithful

Clue 5:

_____ _____ _____ _____ _____

freezing   worry   scowl   riches   outlaw

What's in the bag? _____

What's in the Bag? #4

Read the words on the next page. Then match the letters with the correct synonyms in the clues. (You will not use all the letters.) Put the five clues together and discover what's in the bag!

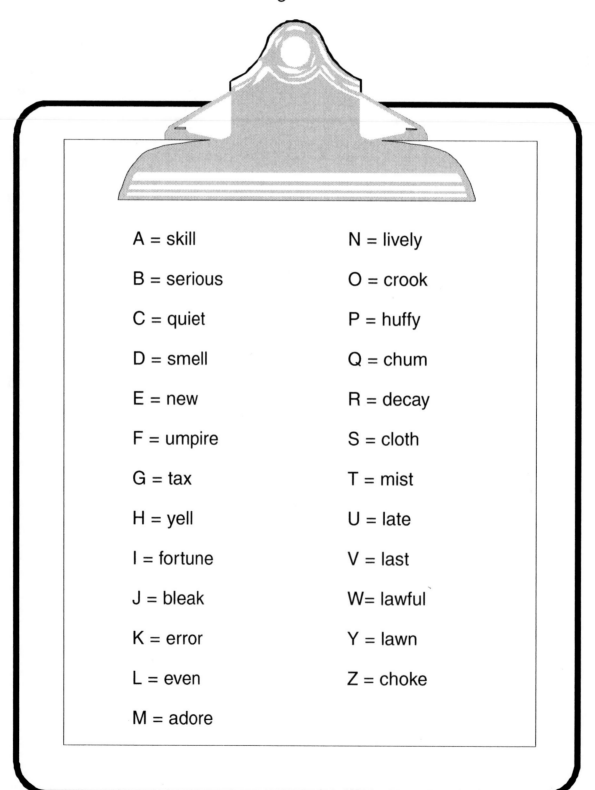

A = skill

B = serious

C = quiet

D = smell

E = new

F = umpire

G = tax

H = yell

I = fortune

J = bleak

K = error

L = even

M = adore

N = lively

O = crook

P = huffy

Q = chum

R = decay

S = cloth

T = mist

U = late

V = last

W = lawful

Y = lawn

Z = choke

What's in the Bag? #4 (cont.)

Clue 1:

_____ _____ _____ _____ _____

calm   shout   novel   legal   grass

Clue 2:

_____ _____ _____ _____ _____

odor   thief   tardy   toll   shout

Clue 3:

_____ _____ _____ _____ _____

grave   art   mistake   novel   odor

Clue 4:

_____ _____ _____ _____ _____ _____

fabric   tardy   toll   art   rot   grass

Clue 5:

_____ _____ _____ _____ _____ _____

odor   thief   gag   novel   spry   fabric

What's in the bag? _____

Banana Split

Split the banana by removing the given letters. Then add the extra letter in and unscramble the word using the clue.

	−	ABN	+	L	=	1. boy's name
		AAB		E		2. girl's name
		ANN		R		3. a person of Arabia
		AAN		D		4. a group of musicians
		AAN		K		5. the side of a river
		AAN		R		6. used in cereal
		AAN		R		7. a farm building
		AB				8. a grandmother

1. _____

2. _____

3. _____

4. _____

5. _____

6. _____

7. _____

8. _____

Extra Points: BANANA + D = an item of headwear

Bicycle Word Search

Lots of bits make up a bike—and they're hidden "wheely well" . . .

Find the following words:

air, bell, bicycle, BMX, chain, gears, light, handlebar, mirror, mudguard,
oil, pedal, pump, seat, spoke, sprocket, tube, tire, valve, wheel

Japanese Words

Find these Japanese words in the puzzle below. The left-over letters spell the special name given to Japanese written characters.

The word is: _____

BAMBOO	NOH (theater)
BUNRAKU (form of puppetry)	ORIGAMI
CHIN (small dog)	SAMISEN (musical instrument)
HAIKU (poem)	SAMPAN (boat)
HARI-KARI (a form of ritual suicide)	SHINTO (religion)
HIROSHIMA	SHO (musical instrument)
JUDO	SUSHI
KABUKI (theater)	TSUNAMI (tidal wave)
KOTO (musical instrument)	YEN (currency)
NIPPON (name for Japan)	

O	R	I	G	A	M	I	N	O	H
T	H	I	R	O	S	H	I	M	A
S	A	M	I	S	E	N	P	I	I
U	R	S	U	S	H	I	P	S	K
N	I	S	D	E	H	X	O	H	U
A	K	A	B	U	K	I	N	O	J
M	A	M	G	C	H	I	N	R	U
I	R	P	K	O	T	O	A	T	D
P	I	A	H	B	A	M	B	O	O
B	U	N	R	A	K	U	Y	E	N

Pair the Pairs

It takes two to duel, or at least a couple, or a twosome. Match up these definitions with their correct pair.

DEFINITIONS

_____ 1. a pair of performers

_____ 2. a performance by two musicians

_____ 3. double

_____ 4. two people closely associated

_____ 5. two rhyming lines of verse

_____ 6. a set of two objects used together

_____ 7. one more than one

_____ 8. two people together

_____ 9. the two on a dice or a playing card

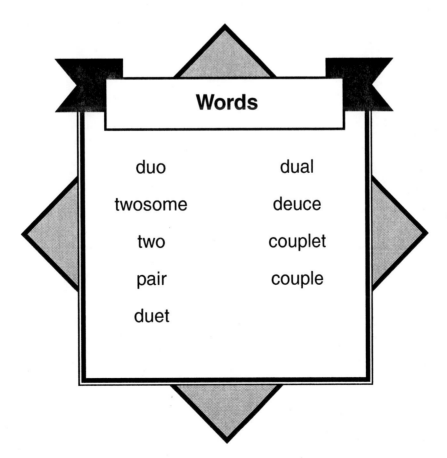

Words

duo	dual
twosome	deuce
two	couplet
pair	couple
duet	

Mars Plus

The Martian moons might have been hard to find, but Mars isn't. It's everywhere. It's hidden in tRAMS and SwARM and MAReS. It's also in every word of today's puzzle!

MARS

1. F +		cultivated lands
2. G +		measures of mass
3. H +		hurts
4. C +		forces or stuffs
5. H +		a swamp
6. O +		wanders
7. W +		heats up
8. P +		sloping paths
9. E +		packets of paper
10. T +		clever

Angling Find-a-Word

Locate the words listed below. The letters left over spell the name of an important fishing manual from the 15th century.

Angle (v): to fish with a hook and line

> angle, cast, fly, freshwater, hook, lakes, line, lure,
> ponds, reel, river, rod, trout, worm

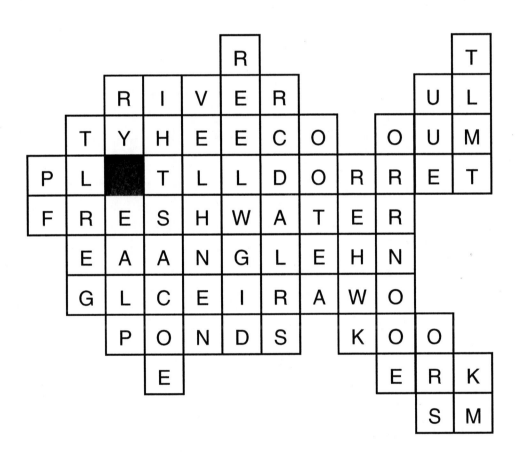

The name of the fishing manual is:

_____

Solve It!

Read the clues and complete the words. Each word only contains letters from the word STRAWBERRY.

1. hits | | | | | S |
2. ready to cry | T | | | |
3. promise | | | | R |
4. skilled | A | | | |
5. scatter | | | | W |
6. animal | B | | | |
7. throw away | | | | E |
8. repeat | R | | | |
9. liquid | | | | R |
10. baking ingredients | Y | | | |

Fruit and Vegetable Circular Puzzle

Here are clues to eight unusual vegetables and fruits. The first word begins with a "T." Each answer begins with the last letter of the preceding word. The last word ends in "T."

1. mildly acid red fruit eaten as a vegetable

2. small oval-shaped European fruit important for food and oil

3. berry-like fruit of the elder shrub

4. the edible root of a tropical vine

5. large, oval, smooth-skinned tropical fruit

6. edible bulb, which causes eyes to sting when peeled

7. smooth-skinned variety of the peach

8. egg-shaped vegetable with a shiny, dark purple skin

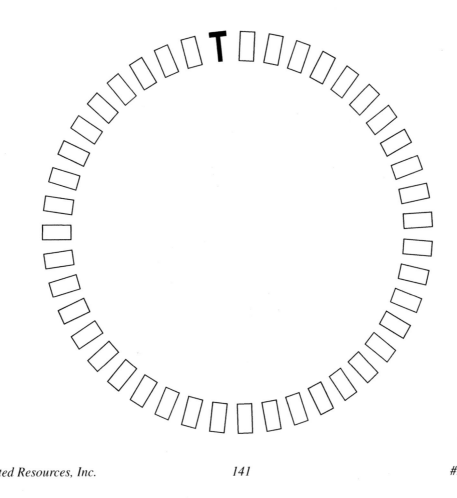

Drive Into This Puzzle!

Cars and films seem to go together so well, but can you turn cars into a film?
Use the clues to help—but you're only allowed to change one letter at a time.

C	A	R	S	
				Rowing implements
				Belonging to us
				Pelts
				Trees
				Combustion
				A steel hand tool
F	I	L	M	

Birds of a Feather

Oh boy! There are bits of birds everywhere! Each bird's name has been split in two—and separated. Join them back to see what's in this flock. P.S. One bird (poor thing) got split into three.

ARD	CO	EON	OST	EN	TURE
PIG	CORM	VUL	PAR	EAG	INAL
CARD	ROT	LE	PECK	ROW	WOOD
CHICK	RICH	ORANT	BUZZ	SPAR	ER

Solar System Word Search

The solar system is a busy place, with planets, the sun, space probes, and satellites. But it's a big place, and sometimes even a planet can be hard to find. Start with a search for these words. The leftover letters will spell out the name of what some scientists believe will be our tenth planet, if we ever find it!

asteroid	gas	meteor	Pluto	Sun
comet	Jupiter	moon	rocket	Uranus
dust	Mars	Neptune	satellite	vacuum
Earth	Mercury	orbit	Saturn	Venus

```
U  E  M  A  R  S  Y  A  P  E  R
R  A  S  E  S  R  S  T  S  U  D
A  R  P  U  U  T  T  I  B  R  O
N  T  N  C  E  N  R  U  T  A  S
U  H  R  R  J  U  P  I  T  E  R
S  E  O  M  E  T  E  O  R  O  V
M  I  T  E  K  C  O  R  H  T  A
D  V  E  N  U  S  O  N  E  U  C
S  A  T  E  L  L  I  T  E  L  U
C  O  M  E  T  N  O  O  M  P  U
G  A  S  E  N  U  T  P  E  N  M
```

Some scientists believe our tenth planet will be called _____.

Henry's Six Wives

Henry's six wives are lost in the spiral! Can you find them all? (*Hint:* He married three Catherines, two Annes, and a Jane.)

_____   _____

_____   _____

_____   _____

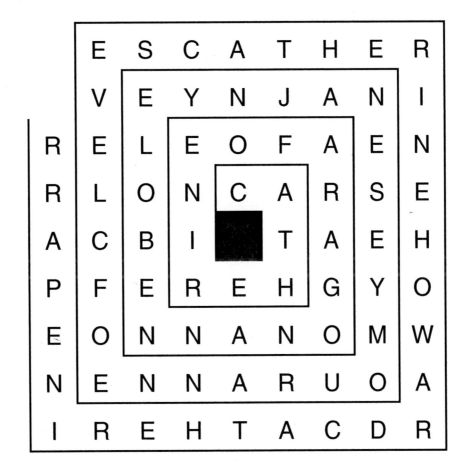

Sand Dune Word Puzzle

Can you make sand into a dune and back into sand by changing one letter at a time?

S	A	N	D
D	U	N	E

D	U	N	E
S	A	N	D

A Colonial Word Search

Test your knowledge of daily life in the 13 colonies. Use these clues to find the 20 words in the word search on page 148.

1. the only sport in which women could participate_____

2. metal from which some plates and cups were made _____

3. the only utensil used for eating _____

4. common method of punishment for criminals _____

5. type of home built by early Dutch settlers _____

6. plant used in making candles _____

7. girls embroidered these _____

8. they sold wares and spread news _____

9. cloth spun from the flax plant_____

10. dish made from wood or stale bread_____

11. children ages six to eight attended these _____

12. plant grown for its blue dye _____

13. windows were made by soaking cloth in this oil _____

14. a basic ingredient of soap _____

15. game in which metal rings were tossed at an iron stake_____

16. one page of letters fastened to a wooden frame_____

17. waist-length jacket worn by men _____

18. fried cornmeal bread _____

19. type of house with sloping roof _____

20. day of worship _____

A Colonial Word Search *(cont.)*

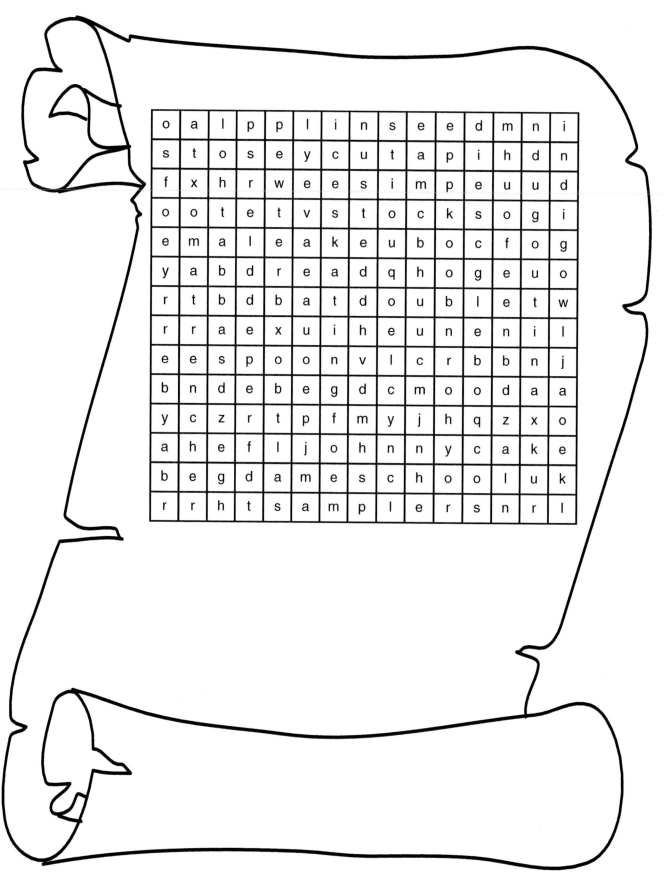

o	a	l	p	p	l	i	n	s	e	e	d	m	n	i
s	t	o	s	e	y	c	u	t	a	p	i	h	d	n
f	x	h	r	w	e	e	s	i	m	p	e	u	u	d
o	o	t	e	t	v	s	t	o	c	k	s	o	g	i
e	m	a	l	e	a	k	e	u	b	o	c	f	o	g
y	a	b	d	r	e	a	d	q	h	o	g	e	u	o
r	t	b	d	b	a	t	d	o	u	b	l	e	t	w
r	r	a	e	x	u	i	h	e	u	n	e	n	i	l
e	e	s	p	o	o	n	v	l	c	r	b	b	n	j
b	n	d	e	b	e	g	d	c	m	o	o	d	a	a
y	c	z	r	t	p	f	m	y	j	h	q	z	x	o
a	h	e	f	l	j	o	h	n	n	y	c	a	k	e
b	e	g	d	a	m	e	s	c	h	o	o	l	u	k
r	r	h	t	s	a	m	p	l	e	r	s	n	r	l

Catch the Elephant

List ways you can think of to catch an elephant that has escaped from the zoo.
Try to think of as many creative and unusual ways as you can.

Pin the Tail on the Words

You'll need to be sharp to work out all these clues—although every answer does begin with a pin.

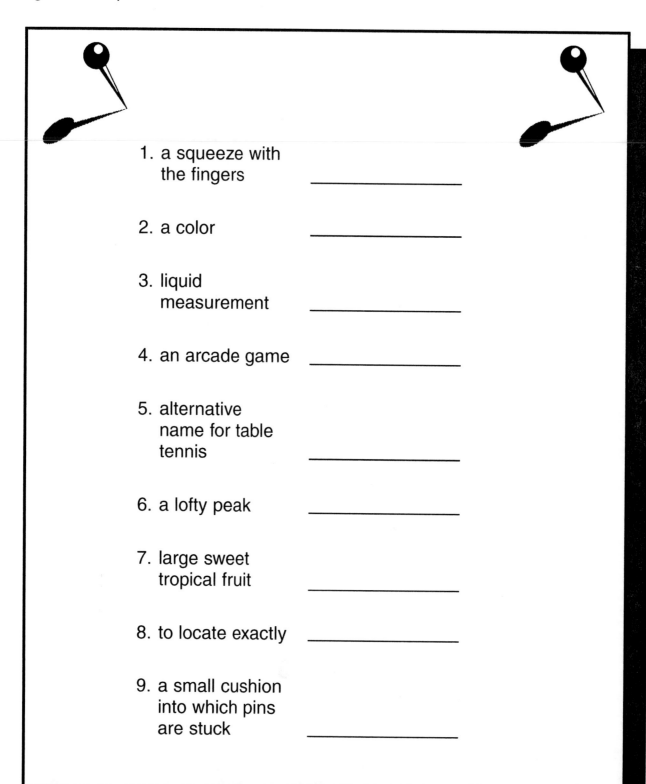

1. a squeeze with the fingers   _____

2. a color   _____

3. liquid measurement   _____

4. an arcade game   _____

5. alternative name for table tennis   _____

6. a lofty peak   _____

7. large sweet tropical fruit   _____

8. to locate exactly   _____

9. a small cushion into which pins are stuck   _____

A Sweet Puzzle

Here are 13 words. Just place them correctly in the squares below and you will have nine types of treats.

AND	IN	POP
BUT	LATE	RICE
CHEW	MALL	SCOT
CORN	MARS	
GUM	OFF	

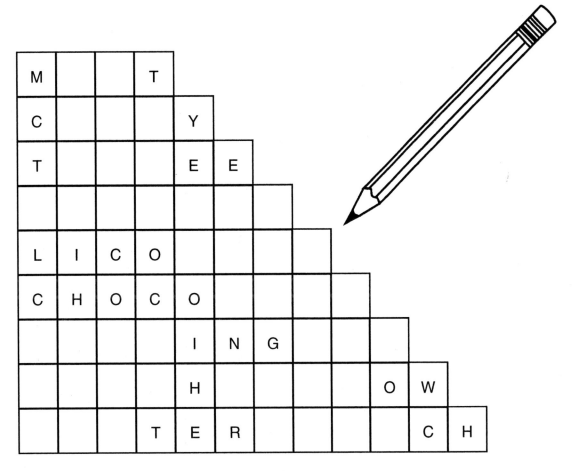

The Big, Bad Wolf

Imagine that the big, bad wolf wants to reform. What advice would you give to help him turn over a new leaf?

_____

_____

_____

_____

_____

_____

_____

_____

_____

_____

_____

_____

_____

Rip Returns!

Imagine that you are a modern-day Rip Van Winkle and go to sleep for 100 years. Describe the world you will find when you awake.

_____

_____

_____

_____

_____

_____

_____

_____

_____

_____

_____

_____

_____

_____

Fantasy Character Conversation

Work with a partner to make up a play about a conversation between different fantasy characters such as Jack from *Jack and the Beanstalk* and Ariel from the *Little Mermaid*.

Now What Happens?

Devise a different ending to *Little Red Riding Hood*.

To the Rescue

Imagine you are living in the magical kingdom of Goth. Your best friend has been captured by a fire-breathing dragon. Write the story of how you rescue him or her. You can use three of the following:

- a flute
- a pair of roller blades
- a magnifying glass
- a packet of bubble gum
- a dog
- a baseball bat

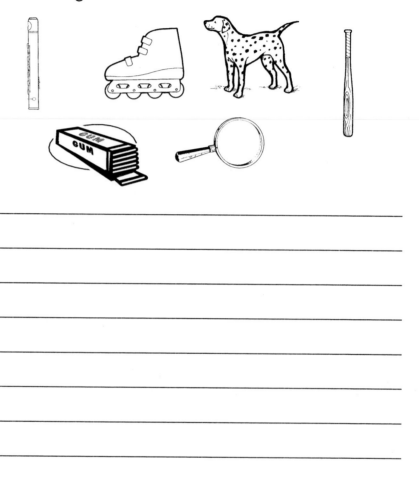

_____

_____

_____

_____

_____

_____

_____

_____

_____

_____

_____

_____

_____

_____

Consequences

What if dinosaurs had not become extinct? Give ten different consequences.

1. _____

2. _____

3. _____

4. _____

5. _____

6. _____

7. _____

8. _____

9. _____

10. _____

Sea Creatures

What kind of sea creature is this?

It has _____ tentacles.

Is it a fish?   Yes / No

Can it breathe underwater? Yes / No

Write a true story about yourself at the beach.

_____

_____

_____

_____

_____

_____

_____

_____

_____

_____

_____

_____

_____

Land With No Gravity

Focus on an imaginary land where there is no gravity. Picture the people; the colors, shapes, sounds and smells; the homes, landscape, buildings, traffic, etc.

What are the people doing? Where are they going?

_____

_____

_____

_____

_____

_____

_____

_____

_____

_____

Ice Cream Poem

Imagine you have been asked to write a poem about ice cream.

Think about the following:

- *The form*—Will it be a limerick, rap, nursery rhyme, prose, chant, or free verse?
- *The structure*—Will it contain similes and metaphors?
- *Visual impact*—Will it be a shape poem or a haiku?

Write the poem.

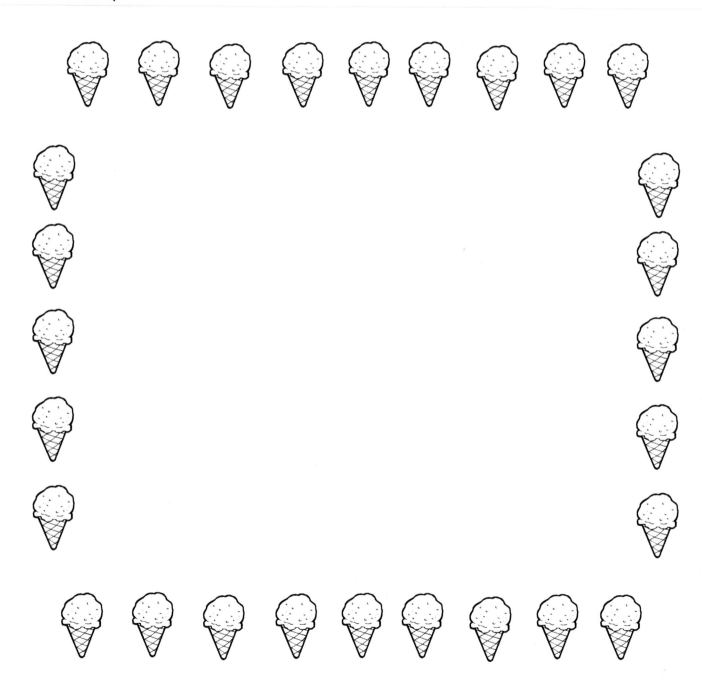

Brainstorm!

Brainstorm the sorts of things that make you laugh.

Brainstorm a list of crazy or far-out things to sell. Examples could be thigs like: birthday parties on the moon, ice cream pizzas, or back-to-front shoes. Challenge yourself to write an advertisement for the product.

Treasure

This treasure chest contains something amazing that has never been seen before on Earth.

What do you imagine it could be? Draw a picture of the treasure and write about it.

_____

_____

_____

_____

_____

What a Question!

This is a happy line leaping and bounding along!

Draw a silly line.

Draw a sad line.

The answer is "no." Write three questions. _____

_____

_____

List reasons why the people were laughing and shouting. _____

_____

You cannot see out of the windows. List the possible reasons why this is so.

_____

_____

_____

Why can't you open the door? Think of possible reasons.

_____

_____

_____

Street Safety

Think of different ways to make your street safer by making cars and other traffic travel more slowly and cautiously. Explain and draw your suggestions.

How Can You Use It?

List possible uses for a milk carton.

_____

_____

_____

_____

_____

_____

_____

How can a piece of string be used for each of these activities or functions?

To play a sport?	To play a game?	An item . . . .

What Can It Be?

This food is shaped like a soccer ball. _____

This food is two colors, one outside and the other inside. _____

This food comes in a bag. _____

You cannot eat this food with a fork. _____

This food makes a noise when it is cooked. _____

List three things that you could never touch.

_____

_____

_____

List three things that you could never wash.

_____

_____

_____

List three things that you could never see at the zoo.

_____

_____

_____

What If?

Explore alternatives by imagining you have the ability to change three things in your life.

What three things would you change?

_____

_____

_____

How would you change them?

_____

_____

_____

_____

How would this affect your life?

_____

_____

_____

_____

Inventing a Robot

Design a robot that will be able to meet your needs in the future. The robot does not have to resemble a person, so you can be very creative. Write a user's manual for your robot, explaining the function or task that each feature of the robot will perform.

_____

_____

_____

_____

_____

_____

_____

My Fun Park

Design and name your own fun park. Write the rules and regulations you feel are important for running the park, and explain why these are necessary. What rides would you have? How would your fun park be different from parks that already exist? What improvements could you make to the existing parks?

My Fun Park *(cont.)*

_____

_____

_____

_____

_____

_____

_____

_____

_____

_____

_____

Stranded

Imagine that all means of transport other than walking are no longer available. Invent new ways of traveling, using items you would be able to find at home or school.

Is That Red?

List or draw all the red objects that you can think of. To be more creative, try to think about the color from a different point of view or as a result of an action, for example: a face blushing or the sun setting.

Finding Categories

Divide these objects into groups with at least two items per group. Label each group with a description, for example, "articles of clothing."

rice	smile	envelope	hat
eggs	cheese	pilot	folder
coin	eyebrows	frown	teacher
scratch	scissors	itch	soldier
wink	legs	box	ears
donut	nail	tin	stamp
toaster	sun	nurse	
beans	rub	rose	

Groups

Recruitment Ad

Imagine you are the most famous artist in the mythical kingdom of Tarambala and you have been asked by your king to design a recruitment ad. The ad is for brave adventurers who are willing to retrieve the precious Golden Orb that has been stolen by fierce pirates.

Design your ad so that all the best and bravest people in the kingdom apply.

Hobbies

List five hobbies for which you would require the following skills:

Physical Strength

_____
_____
_____
_____
_____

Coordination

_____
_____
_____
_____
_____

Creative Thinking

_____
_____
_____
_____
_____

Can you recommend a hobby for these students?

Type of Student	Recommended Hobby	Why Recommended
physically impaired		
visually impaired		
hearing impaired		
inner city dweller		
rural country dweller		
extremely shy person		

Describe the strangest hobby:

_____

_____

_____

Redecorating Your Room

Your parents give you $200 to redecorate your room and you must not make any holes in your walls!

Draw a plan to show how your room will look:

Floor plan of my room	Side view of my room

My color scheme will be the following:

Walls: _____   Curtains: _____

Ceiling: _____   Bedspread: _____

Other items: _____

I have chosen this color scheme because of the following reasons:

_____

_____

Budget for the cost of redecorating my room:

Item	Cost	Item	Cost
		Total Cost =	

If you go over budget with your project, how would you convince your parents to allow you to go ahead with your planned room?

_____

_____

Future Fame

Imagine that you are given the opportunity to become famous. What would you choose to be?

_____

Why would you choose this?

_____

_____

_____

Draw yourself at work.

What would you do in your new life? Where would you go? What results would you hope to achieve?

Write a diary about your first three days of being famous.

Day One: _____

_____

_____

Day Two:_____

_____

_____

Day Three: _____

_____

Moon Colony

You have to lead a moon colonization mission. You can take five people with you to live on the moon. You need to take enough food and supplies to last until you can produce more food. As the leader, you need to establish some rules and consequences.

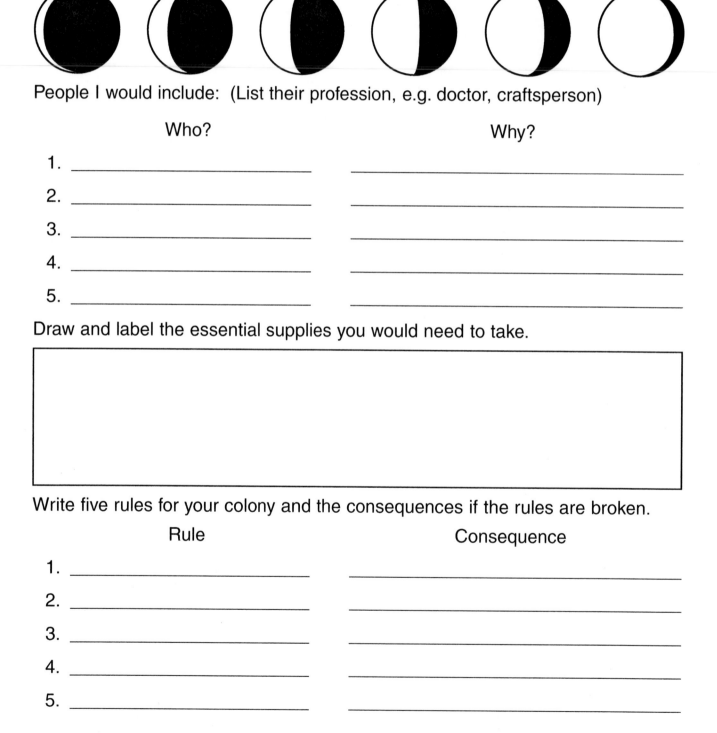

People I would include: (List their profession, e.g. doctor, craftsperson)

Who?	Why?
1. _____	_____
2. _____	_____
3. _____	_____
4. _____	_____
5. _____	_____

Draw and label the essential supplies you would need to take.

Write five rules for your colony and the consequences if the rules are broken.

Rule	Consequence
1. _____	_____
2. _____	_____
3. _____	_____
4. _____	_____
5. _____	_____

Stars and Planets

Circle whether the following statements are true or false.

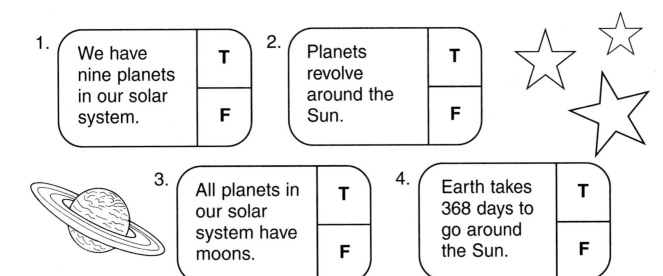

1. We have nine planets in our solar system. T F

2. Planets revolve around the Sun. T F

3. All planets in our solar system have moons. T F

4. Earth takes 368 days to go around the Sun. T F

Illustrate all the true statements.

Write three other TRUE statements about our solar system.

_____

_____

_____

Write three other FALSE statements about our solar system.

_____

_____

_____

Food and Exercise Diary

1. Keep a daily record of what you eat for one week. Complete this table about foods you like to eat.

Foods I should eat and drink often:	Foods I shouldn't eat and drink often:

2. Compare how much time you spend sitting down and how much time you spend doing physical activities. The table below will help you.

Sitting Activities	Mon.	Tues.	Wed.	Thurs.	Fri.	Sat.	Sun.
Reading							
Watching TV							
Studying							
Homework							
At School							
Physical Activities	Mon.	Tues.	Wed.	Thurs.	Fri.	Sat.	Sun.
Games							
Sport							
Walking							
Shopping							

Dream Homes

Choose one of the following home descriptions and design a home.

- • The ideal home for a family with six children.

- • A home suitable for an elderly person.

Show the floor plan for the house. Accompany your plan with some details that explain why you think special features are important.

Use Your Head!

- Imagine you have been transported to the year 3000. Draw a model "television set" of that era.

- Do you agree that young people watch too much television? Give reasons for your answer.

- Television was created to improve communication, but has also been blamed for reducing communication within families. What do you think?

Sand

We find sand at the beach and in rivers. Sand can be coarse or fine. It can be made from particles of shells, rocks, and coral, so it is often different colors.

We have many uses for sand.

- We use it for modeling things like sandcastles at the beach.
- We use it as a filling for soft toys and beanbags.
- Mined sand is used to make glass.

1. Can you think of three other uses for sand?

   A. _____

   B. _____

   C. _____

2. Draw a diagram to help you explain how shells, rocks, and coral are made into grains of sand that are found on the beach or in rivers.

3. In the past, sand was often used to measure time. Design a new device that uses sand to measure time. Illustrate your invention below and describe how it works.

Landmark Match-Up

How's your LIQ (Landmark Intelligence Quotient)? Try matching these famous landmarks to their country of origin.

Who's the Oldest?

News

A reporter from the newspaper was interviewing Old Sam, Old Jack, Old Tom, and Old Angus. "I know all of you are over ninety," said the reporter, "but which of you is the oldest?"

"I'm younger than Old Tom, but older than Old Sam," said Old Jack.

"Eh, what?" said Old Tom.

Old Angus added, to make it clearer, "I'm younger than Old Tom, but older than Old Jack."

"Zzzzz!" snored Old Sam.

Who is the oldest?

Abbreviations

OK is an abbreviation of "okay" that most people recognize. Here are some abbreviations from e-mails and computing. How many can you figure out? Each has a clue to the meaning.

1. WYSIWYG: this will print out how you see it

   _____

2. B4: previously

   _____

3. 2nite: this evening

   _____

4. EZ: not difficult

   _____

5. cuz: for that reason

   _____

6. <g>: smile

   _____

7. <s>: breathe out deeply

   _____

8. THX: expression of gratitude

   _____

9. ROTFL: expressing great amusement

   _____

10. OTOH: alternatively

    _____

11. LTNS: haven't seen you in a while

    _____

12. BTW: introducing a new topic

    _____

13. CU: goodbye

    _____

Top 10 Math

Here's this week's top 10 Rock n' Roll chart. Next to each song is its movement since last week. For example, "Rock Around the Clock" has moved up seven places so it must have been number 8 last week. Use the information to work out all of last week's chart. Who was at the top of the charts?

This Week	Last Week
1. Rock Around the Clock (up 7)	1.
2. Shake, Rattle 'n' Roll (up 8)	2.
3. That'll Be the Day (down 2)	3.
4. Peggy Sue (steady)	4.
5. Love Potion No. 9 (down 2)	5.
6. Wild One (up 3)	6.
7. Run Around Sue (down 2)	7.
8. Heartbreak Hotel (down 2)	8.
9. Shakin' All Over (down 2)	9.
10. Da Doo Ron Ron (down 8)	10.

Which Maze?

To make more money, Tom plans to build a small maze. He draws four designs but can't decide between them. Which design should he choose if he wants his customers to enter and leave from one side? They must go through every door only once.

A

B

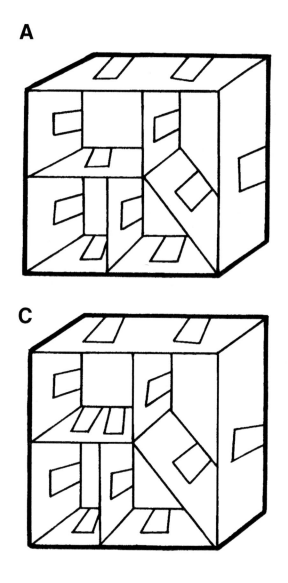

C

D

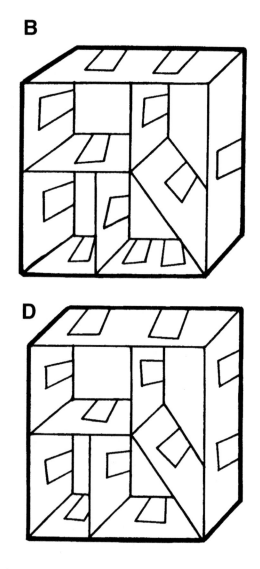

Rhyming Word Pairs

Find an adjective that rhymes with a noun so that together the two words have about the same meaning as the phrase given. An example has been done for you.

Example: a soaked dog = soggy doggy

1. a friend who does not arrive on time _____

2. an overweight rodent_____

3. a naughty boy _____

4. a crude guy _____

5. a beetle's cup _____

6. a lengthy tune _____

7. a plump feline _____

8. twice as much bother _____

9. a large hog _____

10. a girl from Switzerland _____

11. a skinny horse_____

12. a blinding bulb_____

13. a comical rabbit_____

14. a happy boy_____

15. a loafing flower _____

16. an unhappy father _____

17. a home for a rodent_____

18. without money _____

19. an irritated employer _____

20. fake coins _____

IQ Test

Here are 10 questions that are similar to those found in IQ tests. Complete the pattern with the next letter, number, or shape in the pattern.

1. 1, 2, 4, 7, 11, . . . _____

2. 23, 21, 19, 17, . . . _____

3. 1, 4, 9, 16, . . . _____

4. A, C, D, F, G, I, . . . _____

5. Z, A, Y, B, X, C, . . . _____

6. A, E, I, O, . . . _____

7.

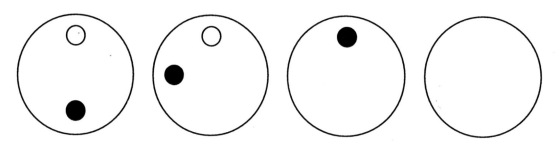

8.

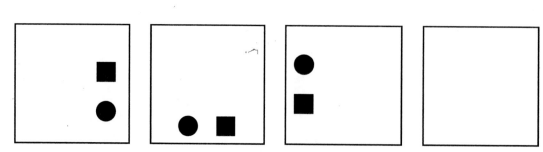

9. I, III, V, VII, . . . _____

10. Which word is least like the other four? cow, bull, sheep, calf, heifer?

_____

Train of Thought

Arrrgh! Disaster is imminent! Locomotive driver Arnie Watson is walking slowly back to the railroad depot along the Spring Gully railroad track. Because he is hearing impared Arnie can't hear the *Spring Gully Express* roaring up directly behind him. He's wearing dark clothing and isn't carrying a lantern. The express had turned off its lights, and there's no moon or stars. There are no lights in this darkly wooded area, yet the Express driver still manages to screech to a halt only meters away from Arnie's back. How?

Picture the Scene

Why is the airplane's arrival delayed? Think of at least five reasons.

_____

_____

_____

_____

_____

How is a cloud like a pillow? List at least eight attributes or characteristics that are similar.

_____

_____

_____

_____

_____

Imagine that all the clocks have stopped. How could this affect you?

_____

_____

_____

_____

_____

More Hidden Meanings

Explain the meaning of each box.

B R
A I N
E D

1. _____

GROUND
FT   FT
FT   FT
FT   FT

2. _____

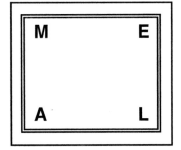

3. _____

knee
light

4. _____

League

5. _____

Man
Campus

6. _____

NEpainCK

7. _____

Check

8. _____

Tim

9. _____

Once
——
Lightly

10. _____

your hat
keep it

11. _____

School

12. _____

Whodunit?

Ah, a case worthy of the great Sherlock Holmes himself! Read the mystery story and see if you can figure out "whodunit."

When Harry left his house it was early on a fine warm day. He fished at his favorite hole for most of the morning, then drove into town to pick up some supplies. It was almost dark when he returned home to discover his home had gone. Vanished. Stolen? Perhaps, but most certainly missing.

At the police station the duty officer was a little bewildered.

"It was there this morning, sir?"

"Yes! Of course it was! Would I not see my own house?"

"Er, were there any tracks—footprints or tire tracks?"

"Only from my vehicle."

"Any other clues that might help us, sir?"

"Well, I had left the fire going, and . . . "

"And what, sir?"

"The ground where it had been was very wet when I got back."

"Ah," said the officer. "That explains it all!"

It does? Can you figure out where Harry's house went?

_____

_____

_____

_____

_____

Crazy Cartoon

Create a cartoon strip which tells about the story of all these unusual characters meeting and having an adventure:

- ◆ Prince Charming with bad breath,

- ◆ Jack and Jill as visitors from outer space,

- ◆ Rapunzel who loves to break dance, and

- ◆ Snow White who is in love with the Gingerbread Man.

Design an ending with a twist.

1	2	3
4	5	6
7	8	9

Brain Challenges

The French Revolutionary Calendar

See if you can calculate what the date of your birthday would be under the calendar adopted by France after the revolution. It had 12 months of 30 days each, and there were 5 days of national holidays from September 17–21.

Summer Months

(starting September 22)

Messidor: the harvesting month

Thermidor: the heat month

Fructidor: the fruit month

Autumn Months

(starting December 21)

Vendémiaire: the vintage month

Brumaire: the fog month

Frimaire: the frost month

Winter Months

(starting March 21)

Nivôse: the snow month

Pluviôse: the rain month

Ventôse: the wind month

Spring Months

(starting June 19)

Germinal: the seeds month

Floréal: the blossoms month

Prairial: the meadows month

According to the French Revolutionary calendar my birthday would be _____.

Follow the Yellow Brick Road

Information

Each brick in the yellow brick road is 30 cm long by 15 cm wide by 10 cm deep.

Each brick weighs 3.5 kg.

Each brick is worth $585.00.

Solve the following problems.

1. How many bricks would be needed to create a path approximately 9 m long by 3 m wide? _____

2. The road to Emerald City is about 40 km long and 3 m wide. How many bricks would be needed for this path? _____

3. What would its area be? _____

4. How much would it cost? _____

5. If the bricks were all piled one on top of the other, how high would the pile be? _____

6. How much would they weigh altogether? _____

The Race

Ali's sponsor, Cheap Stuff for Bikes, has donated a new helmet for the big endurance race. It is not a very good one though. Fifteen kilometers into the race the sponsor's sticker falls off.

For the next 1/4 of the distance it rains, and Ali discovers the helmet isn't waterproof.

The next 1/7 of the distance seems better, although Ali can't see—the helmet's paint has run down her face. Then, the strap breaks and Ali spends the next 1/5 of the distance holding it on with one hand. Ali's helmet falls off, and she spends the last 3/10 of the race hoping the police don't see her. They don't, but she only comes in third. She throws the helmet away.

How long is the race? _____

(Hint: What number has the divisors 4, 7, 5, and 10?)

Orbital Math

Two spacecraft (A and B) are orbiting the earth. They are both traveling at the same speed, but A's orbit takes 90 minutes to complete while B's orbit takes 180 minutes.

1. How many orbits does A complete each day? _____

2. How many orbits does B complete? _____

3. Which satellite is in the higher orbit? _____

4. Both pass over Melbourne, Australia together at 9 A.M. When will they pass over Australia next? _____

5. Spacecraft A is over South America 45 minutes later. Is it day or night? _____

6. How often during the day are the two spacecraft over the same spot? _____

7. Name the satellite that orbits the sun once every 365 days. _____

Leaping Leap Years!

A leap year is a year that is exactly divisible by four. However, if the year is exactly divisible by 100, it is not a leap year. Except, years that are exactly divisible by 400 are leap years.

Which of these years would have been, were, are, or will be leap years? Circle your answers.

1. 1400*

2. 1504*

3. 1600*

4. 1664*

5. 1800

6. 1808

7. 1900

8. 1996

9. 2000

10. 2100

*If leap years had been in use.

Launch Time

It is launch time at the rocket pad. Since there are so many people who speak other languages, the interpreters are translating the countdown into French and Spanish. Unfortunately, somebody's put the countdown into alphabetical rather than reverse numerical order. Can you use your linguistic skills to translate the numbers and then write them in the correct order again?

French	English	Spanish	English
cinq		cero	
deux		cinco	
dix		cuatro	
huit		diez	
neuf		dos	
quatre		nueve	
sept		ocho	
six		seis	
trois		siete	
un		tres	
zero		uno	

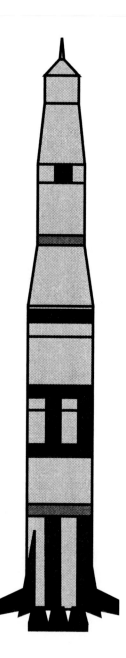

Number Trivia

How many number questions can you answer?

1. Who is code-named Agent 007? _____

2. How many dog years are there for every human year? _____

3. How many years in:

   one decade? _____

   one score? _____

   one century? _____

   one millennium? _____

4. How many cards in a full deck, excluding Jokers? _____

5. What is a 747? _____

6. Who wrote:

   20,000 Leagues Under the Sea? _____

   Around the World in 80 days? _____

   1984? _____

7. Think of three number trivia questions of your own.

   _____

   _____

   _____

20 Questions

The answer is 100. What are 20 questions?

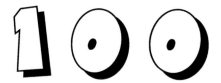

1. _____

2. _____

3. _____

4. _____

5. _____

6. _____

7. _____

8. _____

9. _____

10. _____

11. _____

12. _____

13. _____

14. _____

15. _____

16. _____

17. _____

18. _____

19. _____

20. _____

20 More Questions

The answer is _____ (you choose). What are 20 questions?

1. _____

2. _____

3. _____

4. _____

5. _____

6. _____

7. _____

8. _____

9. _____

10. _____

11. _____

12. _____

13. _____

14. _____

15. _____

16. _____

17. _____

18. _____

19. _____

20. _____

How Many?

How many different ways can you get the correct answer?

You throw a die ten times.

The total number you have to throw is 47.

What numbers could you have thrown to arrive at the right answer?

Everyday Math

Every day we use many different types of mathematical operations. Look at the following activities and write down all the things you would do involving mathematics. An example has been done for you. Write your answers on the next page.

Example

Activity: You go to the store to buy three flavors of ice cream.

Things that involve math:

   a. Find the cost of one ice cream.

   b. Multiply that cost by three.

   c. Check that you have enough money to pay for the ice cream.

   d. Check if you were given the correct change.

---

1. Winning a fishing competition with the biggest fish

2. Deciding which CD to buy—the new release or two at a 20 percent discount

3. Going to the movies by bus

4. Buying two fast food meals

5. Having new carpet installed in your house

6. Buying jeans and a shirt

With a friend, write down all the things you do during the day. Sort them into things that involve math and things that don't.

Things I do that involve math:	Things I do that don't involve math:

Everyday Math *(cont.)*

1. _____

_____

_____

2. _____

_____

_____

3. _____

_____

4. _____

_____

5. _____

_____

_____

6. _____

_____

Lilies

Water lilies double in area every 24 hours. At the beginning of summer there is one water lily on the lake. It takes 60 days for the lake to be completely covered. On what day is it half covered?

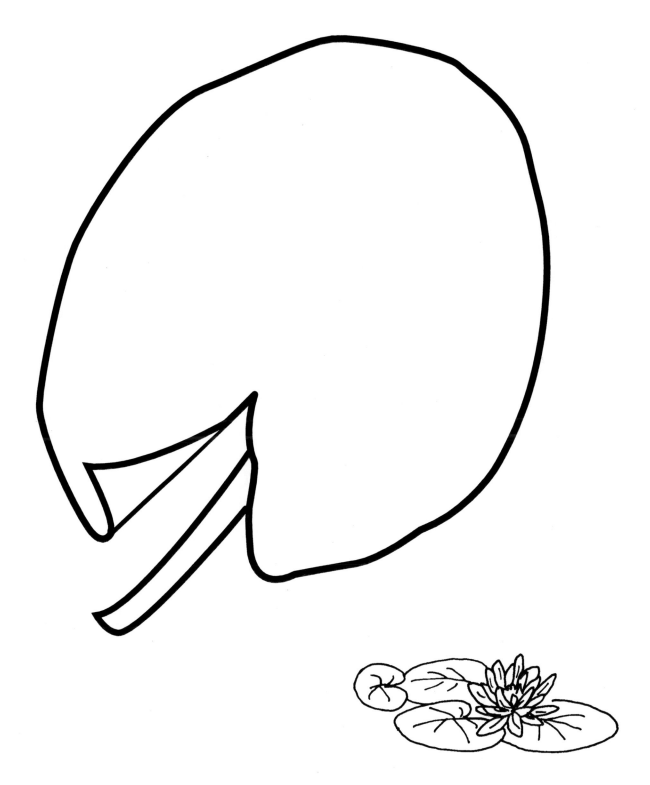

Sam's Solution

Sam worked out that eight nines equal 1125.

He proved to his teacher he was right.

How did he do it?

More How Many?

How many days, hours, and minutes from today until:

New Year's Day?   _____ days

                                      _____ hours

                                      _____ minutes

The Fourth of July   _____ days

                                      _____ hours

                                      _____ minutes

Your 14th birthday   _____ days

                                      _____ hours

                                      _____ minutes

Summer vacation begins   _____ days

                                      _____ hours

                                      _____ minutes

Mother's Day   _____ days

                                      _____ hours

                                      _____ minutes

Fibonacci Numbers

Look at these numbers. They are all in a family called *Fibonacci numbers*. They have a rule that allows them to belong to this family.

Can you figure out the rule to fill in all the blanks?

_____ ,_____ ,_____ ,_____ , 3, 5, 8, 13, 21,_____ ,_____ ,_____ ,_____ ,_____

What is the rule?_____

Fibonacci numbers occur in nature: in pine cones, pineapples, and the petals of many flowers. How many examples can you find that follow this sequence?

What's in a Number?

The name of each of the following objects includes a reference to a number associated with the object. Draw or make a model of each and provide labels.

Write a short description to go with each one.

Tripod	Quintuplets
Unicorn	**Binoculars**
Octopus	**Centipede**
Hexapod	**Dodecahedron**

Let's Go Shopping

Four friends spent the day shopping at a clothing store. From the clues given below, determine how much each spent and which item she purchased. Use an "O" for the correct answers and an "X" for the incorrect answers.

1. The skirt cost more than the shirt but less than the dress and shorts.
2. Shari spent more than Jenna or Margaret but less than the person who bought the dress.
3. Jenna spent more than Margaret.

	dress	shirt	skirt	shorts	$11.00	$20.00	$25.00	$30.00
Shari								
Rhonda								
Jenna								
Margaret								

An Ancient Problem

There once was a king who had a great kingdom and great riches. The king discovered a young scholar who showed great promise. He offered the young scholar half of his kingdom or one grain of wheat on a chessboard doubled for every square. What do you suppose the young scholar chose?

Make this ancient problem more meaningful to you by solving the following problem: Someone has offered you a million dollars or one penny doubled for every square of a checkerboard. The board is drawn below. Use the checkerboard and some paper to calculate which is the better choice.

Write your decision here: _____

_____

_____

_____

Numerical Palindromes

A palindrome is a word, phrase, or number that is the same when it is read frontwards or backwards. Words like toot and dad are simple palindromes. "A Toyota" and "Madam, I'm Adam" are examples of phrases that are palindromes. Numbers like 1221 and 576675 are numerical palindromes.

NOON

MOM   12321

401104   DID

The following is a method to generate a numerical palindrome.

1. Start with any four-digit number.	1563
2. Reverse the digits.	3651
3. Add the original number.	$1563 + 3651 = 5214$
4. Reverse the digits.	4125
5. Add the numbers.	$5214 + 4125 = 9339$

This is a palindrome!

Do this for six different numbers to test the process. The number of times that you will have to repeat the process of reversing and adding will vary. Can you find another way to produce palindromes?

Supermarket Competition

These are the four finalists' shopping carts in the local supermarket's "Dash for Cash" competition. They had just one minute to fill their carts with cash. How much did each finalist get, and who won? Use the chart to determine how much each cart collected. For example, cart 1 collected 33 five dollar bills, which equals $165.00.

Bills	Cart 1	Cart 2	Cart 3	Cart 4
$5	33	5	26	11
$10	10	15	8	12
$20	5	8	8	12
$50	4	5	4	5
$100	4	5	4	5
Totals				

Show your work here.

Who Won? _____

Missing Numbers

The missing numbers in this puzzle are the digits 1 to 9. Each digit is used only once. Complete the puzzle using the clues below.

Columns

? ?
?

? ?

	A	B	C	
A			14	?
B			15	**Totals**
C			16	?
Totals	14	15	16	

Rows

?

? ?
?

Totals

? ?

Clues

✎ Row A has all even digits.

✎ 4 and 6 are in the same column.

✎ 1 and 9 are in the same row.

✎ Row B has all odd digits.

✎ 6 is not in the same row as 4.

Handshakes

There are eight people at a party. If every person shakes hands with everyone else at the party, how many handshakes will there be? _____

Show your work and explain your answer.

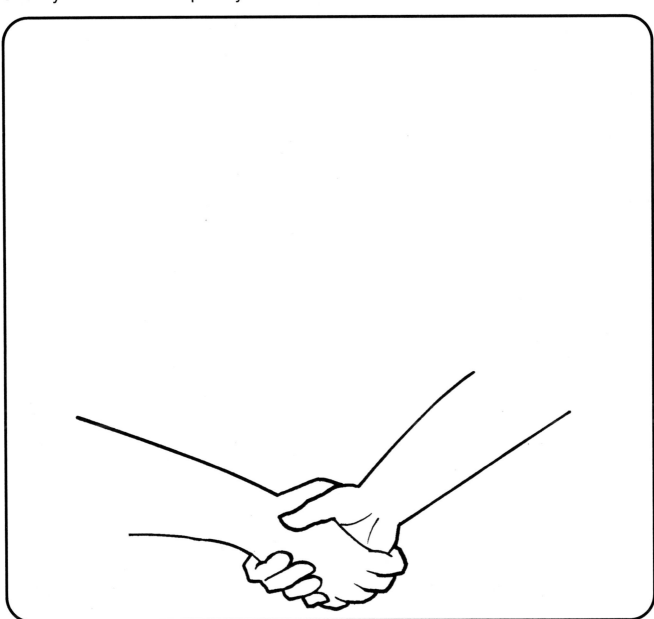

Extension: How many handshakes would there be in your family? _____

What's in the Bag? #5

Read the words on the next page. Then match the letters with the correct synonyms in the clues. (You will not use all the letters.) Put the five clues together and discover what's in the bag!

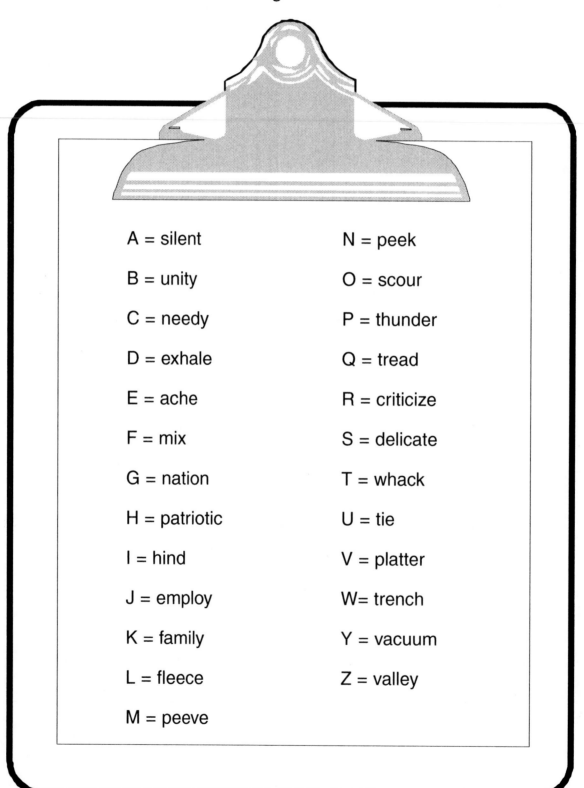

A = silent

B = unity

C = needy

D = exhale

E = ache

F = mix

G = nation

H = patriotic

I = hind

J = employ

K = family

L = fleece

M = peeve

N = peek

O = scour

P = thunder

Q = tread

R = criticize

S = delicate

T = whack

U = tie

V = platter

W = trench

Y = vacuum

Z = valley

What's in the Bag? #5 (cont.)

Clue 1:

_____ _____ _____ _____ _____ _____

rumble   mute   breathe   breathe   hurt   breathe

Clue 2:

_____ _____ _____ _____ _____

loyal   hurt   mute   wool   tender

Clue 3:

_____ _____ _____ _____ _____ _____

rear   glance   hire   knot   scold   sweep

Clue 4:

_____ _____ _____ _____ _____ _____

tender   club   rear   poor   kin   sweep

Clue 5:

_____ _____ _____ _____ _____

tender   club   scold   rear   rumble

What's in the bag? _____

What's in the Bag? #6

Read the words on the next page. Then match the letters with the correct synonyms in the clues. (You will not use all of the letters.) Put the five clues together and discover what's in the bag!

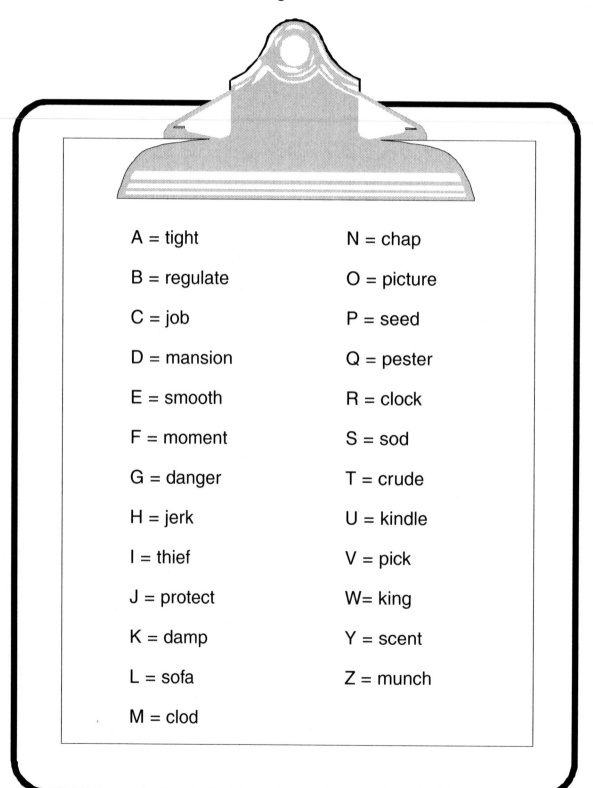

A = tight	N = chap
B = regulate	O = picture
C = job	P = seed
D = mansion	Q = pester
E = smooth	R = clock
F = moment	S = sod
G = danger	T = crude
H = jerk	U = kindle
I = thief	V = pick
J = protect	W = king
K = damp	Y = scent
L = sofa	Z = munch
M = clod	

What's in the Bag? #6 *(cont.)*

Clue 1:

_____   _____   _____   _____   _____   _____

hazard   taut   palace   peril   silky   coarse

Clue 2:

_____   _____   _____   _____   _____   _____

choose   crook   silky   ruler   silky   timer

Clue 3:

_____   _____   _____   _____   _____   _____   _____   _____

career   twitch   taut   fellow   fellow   silky   couch   grass

Clue 4:

_____   _____   _____   _____   _____   _____   _____   _____

portrait   grain   silky   timer   taut   coarse   silky   grass

Clue 5:

_____   _____

coarse   choose

What's in the bag? _____

What's in the Bag? #7

Read the words on the next page. Then match the letters with the correct synonyms in the clues. (You will not use all of the letters.) Put the five clues together and discover what's in the bag!

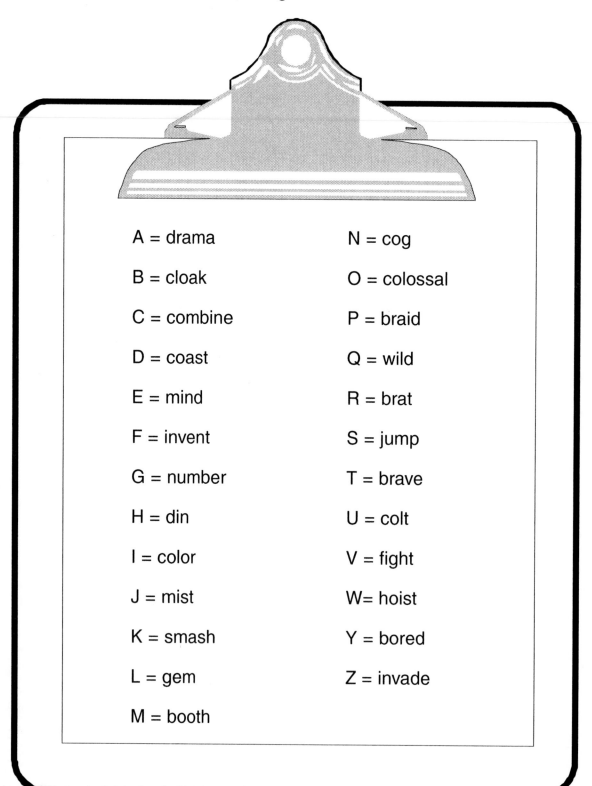

A = drama

B = cloak

C = combine

D = coast

E = mind

F = invent

G = number

H = din

I = color

J = mist

K = smash

L = gem

M = booth

N = cog

O = colossal

P = braid

Q = wild

R = brat

S = jump

T = brave

U = colt

V = fight

W= hoist

Y = bored

Z = invade

What's in the Bag? #7 *(cont.)*

Clue 1:

_____ _____ _____ _____ _____ _____ _____

weave   rascal   hue   battle   play   bold   brain

Clue 2:

_____ _____ _____ _____

brain   play   rascal   skip

Clue 3:

_____ _____ _____ _____ _____ _____ _____

mix   play   rascal   rascal   hue   brain   skip

Clue 4:

_____ _____ _____ _____ _____

stall   horse   skip   hue   mix

Clue 5:

_____ _____ _____ _____

mix   jewel   play   stall   weave

What's in the bag? _____

What's in the Bag? #8

Read the words on the next page. Then match the letters with the correct synonyms in the clues. (You will not use all of the letters.) Put the five clues together and discover what's in the bag!

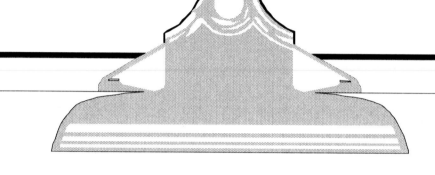

A = signal

B = point

C = blaze

D = space

E = bargain

F = anxious

G = club

H = coarse

I = complete

J = gloomy

K = destroy

L = dissolve

M = anchor

N = cog

N = evening

O = droop

P = practice

Q = entertain

R = electrify

S = follower

T = excuse

U = faith

V = exotic

W = fleet

Y = rural

Z = biscuit

What's in the Bag? #8 (cont.)

Clue 1:

_____ _____ _____ _____ _____ _____

rough   alarm   dusk   area   melt   sale

Clue 2:

_____ _____ _____ _____ _____

fan   dock   alarm   fire   ruin

Clue 3:

_____ _____ _____ _____ _____ _____

ships   finish   dusk   group   sale   area

Clue 4:

_____ _____ _____ _____ _____ _____

finish   dusk   fan   sale   fire   forgive

Clue 5:

_____ _____ _____

rough   finish   forgive

What's in the bag? _____

Procrastination Rules!

Here's a bunch of scrambled words that all mean to procrastinate, delay, hold back, or ignore. How many of them can you find? Or should you just put it all off until later?

FFO-TUP	RINLGE	EMIPED	ROITEL
DEEFR	NETIDA	DRIHEN	OOOVERKL
PONESTOP	TRESRA	DELWAD	SSUPDEN
TINDISCONUE	TLALS	YATS	

How Sharp Are You Today?

You can change "blunt" into "sharp" in 13 steps! Read each clue then change just one letter of the previous answer to make the new word.

B	L	U	N	T	
					The main force of a blow
					A low, pig-like noise
					Let have
					$1000
					A heated iron
					Has no taste or flavor
					Empty, not written in
					A straight length of wood
					To put seeds in the ground
					Not level
					Abbreviation of "shall not"
					Boy's name
					To give out a fair portion
S	H	A	R	P	

Constellation Word Search

Find and circle the words in the word search that are in the box. All of the words are the names of constellations.

Aquarius	Capricorn
Libra	Scorpio
Aries	Gemini
Pisces	Taurus
Cancer	Leo
Sagittarius	Virgo

```
S   U   R   U   A   T   A   U   S   T   R

V   I   R   G   O   A   L   I   A   S   S

C   A   P   R   I   C   O   R   N   O   P

U   A   R   B   I   L   T   H   E   R   I

S   A   G   I   T   T   A   R   I   U   S

N   S   U   I   R   A   U   Q   A   O   C

S   C   O   R   P   I   O   C   R   E   E

O   S   R   E   C   N   A   C   S   L   S

G   E   M   I   N   I   S   E   I   R   A
```

Your Name

Write all of the letters of your first and last name. How many words of three or more letters can you make from your name?

_____

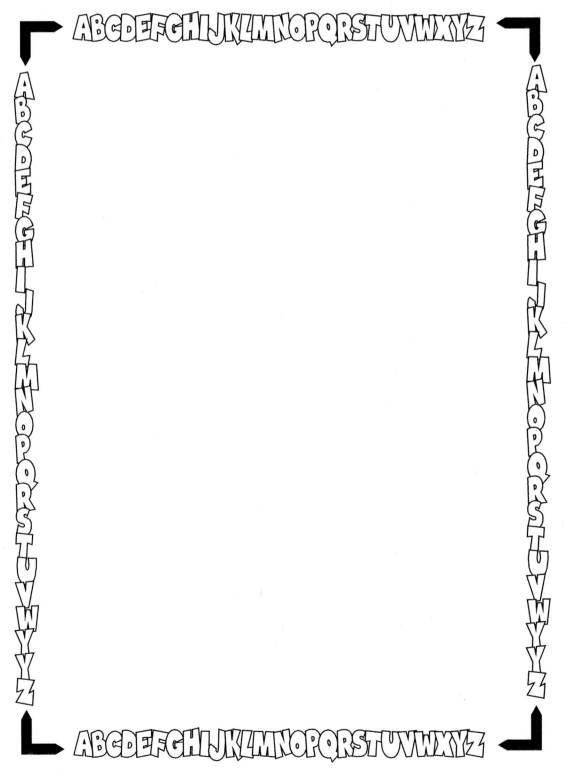

Jumbled Music Styles

Remove the indicated letters and then unscramble the remaining letters to spell out a musical style. (example: AWNINGS – AN = WINGS = swing)

1. BUGLES – G = _____

2. CHIP SHOP – CS = _____

3. CODFISH – FH = _____

4. CROAK – A = _____

5. CRYING OUT – GI = _____

6. FLOCK – C = _____

7. HIPPO – HI = _____

8. LOCK, STOCK, AND BARREL – ABCEKST = (three words) _____

    _____

9. MISCALCULATES – EMTU = _____

10. NOTCHED – D = _____

11. THAMES VALLEY – LS = (two words) _____

12. UNPACK – AC = _____

Style Search

Rock, jazz, classical, country, gospel . . . the list of musical styles can seem never-ending. Here's a list of 22 styles. Find them all, and the leftover letters will spell out the names of four other styles that are thought to have come together to create rock and roll.

be bop, bluegrass, blues, country, dance, disco,
Dixieland, gospel, grunge, heavy metal, heavy
rock, hip hop, rap, rave, rock, rock and roll, speed,
metal, surf, swing, synth pop

B D N A L E I X I D O S P H O G

R O C K A N D R O L L P O E L E

C O U N T R Y I E W O E P A E G

E G E K E P O H P I H E H V P N

C N V C M O G I E S J D T Y S U

N I A O Y U M P B E L M N R O R

A W R R V U E F R U S E Y O G G

D S S S A R G E U L B T S C S R

D P O B E B O O W B O A P K A H

O N K Y H D I S C O T L O P N K

The four other styles: _____ _____

_____ _____

Across-Word

Though this puzzle is less than witty, low on fun and jollity,
a plus is in its brevity, and that each word must end in "ity."

Energy from electrons

								i	t	y

An object's ability

							i	t	y

Steadiness

							i	t	y

The smaller of two groups

						i	t	y

The attractive force of the earth

					i	t	y

A game or pursuit

					i	t	y

Being long-lived

						i	t	y

Quality of being admired

							i	t	y

Being sensitive

							i	t	y

The Clipper Ship Crossword

1. A ship's living quarters

2. Where food is cooked

3. Left (direction)

4. The back of a ship

5. A ship's body

6. The front of a ship

7. They leave a sinking ship

8. Dropped to keep a ship from moving

9. Replaces sails on modern ships

10. Right (direction)

What is the special name for a mariner who sailed around the tip of South America?

Bulb Additions

Add "bulb" to the letter *r*. Rearrange into a promotional statement on a book jacket and you have a "blurb." Can you complete these nine other "bulb additions"?

bulb + ae = an ornament

bulb + be = a hollow globule of gas

bulb + eh = an orbiting space telescope

bulb + er = the remains of a broken building

bulb + cde = to have been hit with a heavy stick

bulb + eiq = to argue over a small item

bulb + adeer = a famous pirate

bulb + begmu = a kind of chewing gum

Con Job

Every answer to these clues begins with "con"—and all the letters can be found in Constantinople. What a convenient word!

solid shape with a circular base rising to a point

◯ ◯ ◯ ◯

agree to

◯ ◯ ◯ ◯ ◯ ◯

to comfort a sad person

◯ ◯ ◯ ◯ ◯ ◯ ◯

keep within a boundary

◯ ◯ ◯ ◯ ◯ ◯ ◯

happy

◯ ◯ ◯ ◯ ◯ ◯ ◯

competition between rivals

◯ ◯ ◯ ◯ ◯ ◯ ◯

uninterrupted

◯ ◯ ◯ ◯ ◯ ◯ ◯ ◯

a speech sound that is not a vowel

◯ ◯ ◯ ◯ ◯ ◯ ◯ ◯ ◯

a large land mass

◯ ◯ ◯ ◯ ◯ ◯ ◯ ◯ ◯

Buttery Words

Butter certainly crops up in all manner of places, recipes, and words—so read the clues and work out these buttery words!

B U T T E R +	I	=	1. a special TV show honoring a person
	EN		2. a person with brown hair
	SS		3. a stone support for a building
	NO		4. to button again
	JO		5. a type of engine
	EIQ		6. a charcoal fuel block
	CPU		7. a flower
	GIL		8. someone who litters
	GIJ		9. a dance from the '50s
	CGSY		10. a famous battle of the Civil War

1. _____

2. _____

3. _____

4. _____

5. _____

6. _____

7. _____

8. _____

9. _____

10. _____

All Roads Lead to Rome

Here are eight roads leading to Rome. The names are scrambled but you know that each one contains the letters "R-O-M-E." Use the clues to identify each road.

1. Old-fashioned women's underpants
2. A tropical plant often found in a swamp.
3. Someone who pays for goods or services.
4. A person who employs people.
5. A person who creates original music.
6. Very large
7. Examined and noted similarities and differences
8. The mathematics of points, lines, curves, and surfaces.

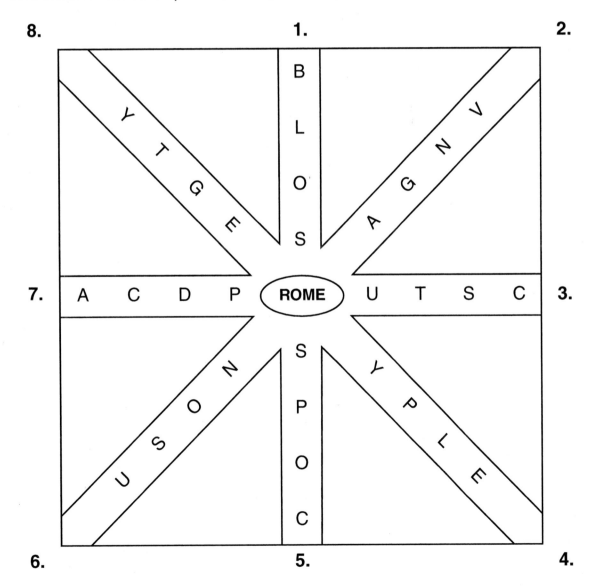

Leo's Likes and Dislikes

The following are some questions using made-up facts about Leonardo Da Vinci. Leonardo Da Vinci liked the shape of an OVAL but not a SQUARE; he invented the ROAD but not the PATH; he liked to LEND money but not BORROW it. Using his name as a clue, try to answer the questions.

1. Paint a DANDELION or a ROSE? _____

2. Predict GLOBAL WARMING or ACID RAIN? _____

3. Invent the AIRLINE or the TRAIN? _____

4. Invent the THEATER or the DRIVE-IN? _____

5. Design the RADIO or the TV? _____

6. Make RADIAL or CROSS-PLY tires? _____

7. Make a CRADLE or a CRIB? _____

8. Invent COMPUTER games or ARCADE games? _____

9. Draw a portrait of an ALIEN or a BIGFOOT? _____

10. Invent the CASSETTE or the VIDEO? _____

My Turn to be a Hero

The letters A–Z are written on this page and the next page. For each letter, think of a situation in which you could become a hero. For example: Avalanche—I could help to rescue someone from beneath the snow.

A _____

B _____

C _____

D _____

E _____

F _____

G _____

H _____

I _____

J _____

K _____

L _____

M _____

My Turn to be a Hero (cont.)

N _____

O _____

P _____

Q _____

R _____

S _____

T _____

U _____

V _____

W _____

X _____

Y _____

Z _____

Complete a Word

Use the 26 letters of the alphabet to complete the words below. Use each letter only one time. (*Hint:* Cross off the letters as you use them.) Write what the word means on the line below.

| a b c d e f g h i j k l m |
| n o p q r s t u v w x y z |

1. ○ u i d e

_____

2. ○ c c o ○ d ○ o n

_____

3. s c r a ○ ○ ○ e

_____

4. a ○ u e ○ u c t

_____

5. ○ u f ○ i ○

_____

6. ○ ○ e s s

_____

7. ○ a ○ n

_____

8. s ○ r ○ e ○

_____

9. e x c ○ r p t

_____

10. s c o r p i ○ ○

_____

11. ○ i ○ h e r

_____

12. ○ u n ○

_____

Palindrome Word Find

Palindromes are words, phrases, sentences, or numbers that read the same forward and backward. Two examples are *121* and *Anna.* See how many palindromes you can find in this puzzle. (There are 34 words in all.)

```
S  J  B  L  A  D  B  B  U  O  F  M  B  E  W  E  Z  C
L  O  P  E  A  C  O  I  D  L  N  U  N  T  R  H  N  H
E  C  O  E  C  B  Q  O  B  J  T  M  M  O  E  A  B  T
V  T  M  Y  E  P  D  K  P  K  N  L  T  A  O  N  P  B
E  O  O  L  Z  P  M  H  E  V  E  I  Q  D  D  N  E  A
L  X  W  T  U  X  N  A  T  S  Q  M  T  H  I  A  E  T
A  T  J  P  S  R  N  U  Y  Z  K  A  R  S  T  H  M  X
N  A  D  D  B  D  R  R  Z  P  L  J  O  O  U  Q  O  J
J  Z  S  O  Z  I  A  T  K  W  O  H  A  L  T  R  X  O
D  E  E  D  M  G  D  A  B  S  S  P  W  O  C  O  L  T
B  Y  A  O  A  M  A  G  K  V  A  L  P  S  I  K  R  T
T  E  R  A  N  X  R  G  W  D  G  Z  F  R  V  G  V  O
E  A  R  K  N  L  S  L  O  I  A  L  U  P  I  K  M  O
R  E  P  A  P  E  R  U  W  D  S  N  I  O  C  M  O  T
R  X  H  Y  S  X  P  S  N  J  E  O  N  T  E  R  M  G
E  O  K  A  F  O  I  U  D  U  D  M  B  A  C  E  B  I
T  H  A  K  D  J  M  N  X  R  G  H  E  W  C  A  B  T
S  E  E  S  U  N  X  W  O  A  L  S  K  A  G  Z  P  O
```

244

More Letter Answers

Use one, two, or three letters of the alphabet to "spell" a word corresponding to each of the following clues. The first one has been done for you.

1. Used in a pool game   Q

2. Happiness   _____

3. A foe   _____

4. Jealousy   _____

5. A woman's name   _____

6. In debt   _____

7. A written composition   _____

8. What makes a movie exciting _____

9. A boy's name   _____

10. To say good-bye   _____

11. The number after 79   _____

12. A drink, hot or iced   _____

13. An exclamation   _____

14. To be good at something   _____

15. To rot   _____

Tutu Entanglement

What would we do without tutus? We would not have any of the following words or phrases, that's for sure! Add TUTU to the letters below and then unscramble them using the clue.

TUTU + ERBENPTA AND JELLY = <u>PEANUT BUTTER</u>
                     (Clue)

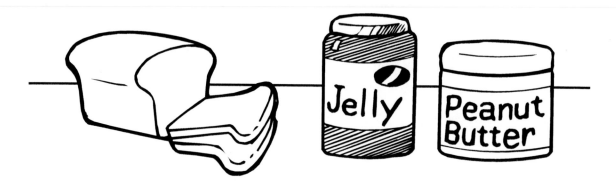

		clue	word or phrase
T U T U +	OP	things produced	
	RON	attendance for an event	
	HNR	a lie	
	PREB	to flatter	
	ROBS	sudden violent happening	
	BIMK	a city in Africa	
	FLHR	honest	
	ABNOR	rotate through a half circle	
	PRECB	flower	
	EFOON	unmusical	

Alphabet Elevator

At the alphabet convention, letters using the elevator have to arrange themselves into words. Use the clues and figure out what words the letters made on each floor.

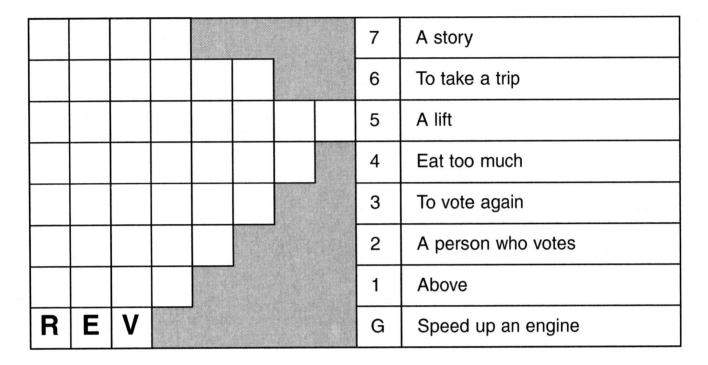

							7	A story
							6	To take a trip
							5	A lift
							4	Eat too much
							3	To vote again
							2	A person who votes
							1	Above
R	E	V					G	Speed up an engine

V, E, and R get in the elevator on the ground floor.

On the first floor, O joins them.

T gets in on the second floor.

E's twin (E) joins them on floor 3.

A hurries in on the 4th floor.

L gets in on the 5th floor—the elevator is full!

O and E get out on the 6th floor.

V and R get out on the 7th floor.

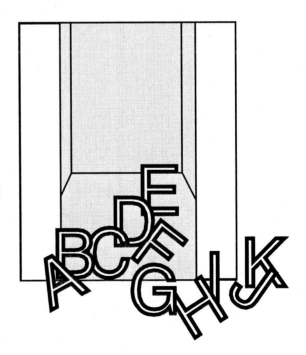

Symphony Orchestra Word Search

Find all these instruments in the word search below. The leftover letters will tell you what the musician standing out in front of the orchestra has to do.

alto clarinet, bass clarinet, bassoon, cello, cor anglais, double bass, flute, French horn, gong, piano, piccolo, snare, timpani, triangle, trombone, trumpet, tuba, viola, violin

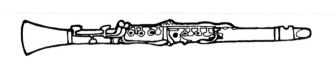

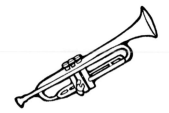

```
O N A I P G N O G C V T S T
O N I N A P M I T D I U S R
F R E N C H H O R N O B A O
T E N I R A L C O T L A B M
S I A L G N A R O C A U E B
B A S S C L A R I N E T L O
T R I A N G L E T U L F B N
T R U M P E T C E L L O U E
P I C C O L O B A S S O O N
V I O L I N S N A R E C D T
```

What does the musician standing out in front of the orchestra do? _____

Jelly Legs

Imagine that your body is made of jelly. List everyday things you would not be able to do, and how your jelly body would affect your daily activities. What would you be able to do that you can't do with your current body?

Hammurabi's Codes

Hammurabi, King of Mesopotamia in about 1792 B.C., brought great changes to the laws of his country. Two of his laws were the following:

1. Wrongdoers were judged and punished by the decision of the society, rather than by the victim and/or the victim's family.

2. All killings were treated as murder.

List the advantages and the disadvantages of these two laws.

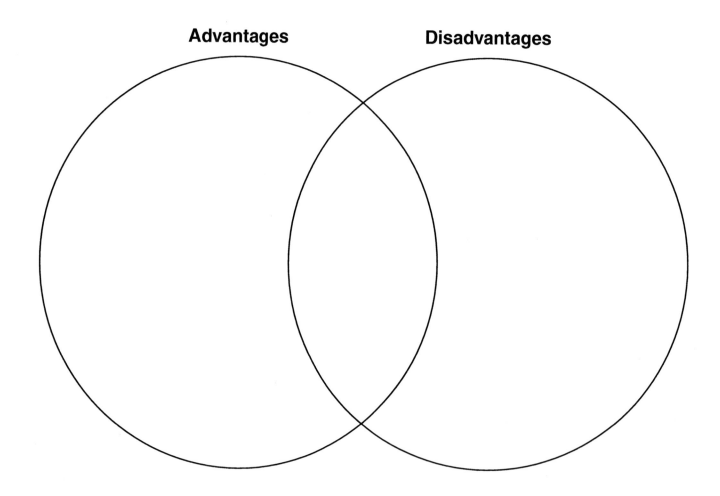

Advantages   **Disadvantages**

Funny Books

Identify what makes a book or character funny.

Name some of the humorous books you have read.

My Hero

From all of the people you have ever known, read about, or heard about choose one person who impresses you most.

Write a haiku or limerick about this person.

Morse Code

Here is what Morse code looks like. It sounds like this: dot = quick sound or tap, dash = longer sound. Using Morse code, write a note to a friend using only the dots and dashes of the code. Be sure to allow enough space between each letter so that the letters don't run into each other. Write your letter on the next page.

Morse Code

A ●▬	B ▬●●●	C ▬●▬●	D ▬●●	E ●	F ●●▬●
G ▬▬●	H ●●●●	I ●●	J ●▬▬▬	K ▬●▬	L ●▬●●
M ▬▬	N ▬●	O ▬▬▬	P ●▬▬●	Q ▬▬●▬	R ●▬●
S ●●●	T ▬	U ●●▬	V ●●●▬	W ●▬▬	X ▬●●▬
Y ▬●▬▬	Z ▬▬●●	1 ●▬▬▬▬	2 ●●▬▬▬	3 ●●●▬▬	4 ●●●●▬
5 ●●●●●	6 ▬●●●●	7 ▬▬●●●	8 ▬▬▬●●	9 ▬▬▬▬●	0 ▬▬▬▬▬

period ●▬●▬●▬	comma ▬▬●●▬▬	? ●●▬▬●●	SOS ●●●▬▬▬●●●		Start ▬●▬

End of Message ●▬●▬●	Understand ●▬●	Error ●●●●●●●●

Morse Code *(cont.)*

Write your letter here.

_____

_____

_____

_____

_____

_____

_____

_____

_____

_____

City Link

Each of these cities begins with the last letter of the previous answer. Join them up in one long city link.

1. Previous U.S. capital

2. Capital of Kuwait

3. Capital of Japan

4. Capital of Norway

5. Capital of Canada

6. Capital of Greece

7. Capital of South Korea

8. Capital of England

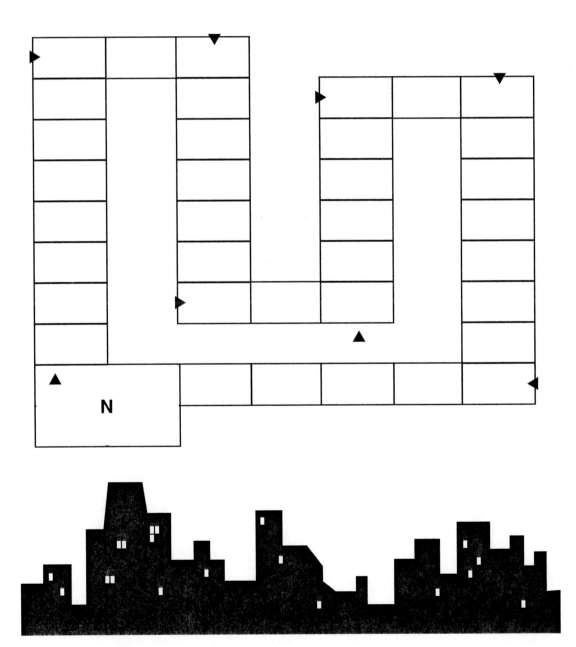

255

Stunt Puzzle

Jim Band is a hero in movies. In his latest movie, the hero is forced to escape from a maze. While escaping, Jim Band (or at least his stunt double) must do the following:

- Wrestle a lion
- Escape from ropes
- Jump from a building (it's a big maze)
- Carry a bomb
- Swim in shark-infested water
- Swing beneath a bridge
- Jump a double-decker bus (okay, it's a really BIG maze!)

He must enter via the North entrance, and in completing all of these stunts, he must cover every path but not travel the same path twice.

1. Where does the stunt double exit? _____

2. In what order are the stunts done? _____

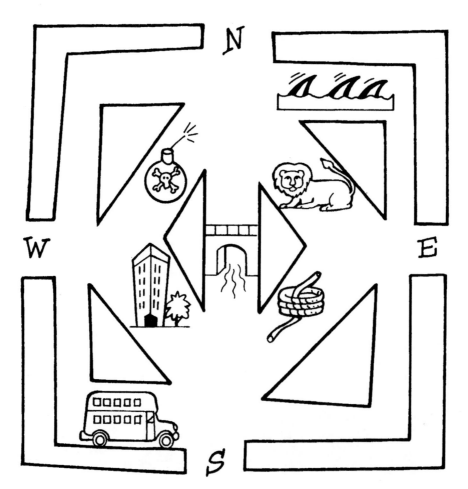

Muddled (and Endangered) Creatures

Look at this list of animals. Do the names seem unfamiliar? If they're not saved from extinction, then children 100 years from now may find the real names unfamiliar, too. So, unscramble them and find the names of 11 endangered mammals, reptiles, and birds.

raptor_____

hateech _____

conrod_____

roodiccle _____

pheelnat _____

leglaze_____

orchesrion _____

lutter _____

halwe_____

poorweekcd_____

Be Creative

Design a device in the box that will save time by doing something that is normally done manually (by hand). Explain how it will work.

Detailed explanation of how the device will work:

_____

_____

_____

_____

Using Technology

Name all of the machines that you could possibly use during an average day.

_____

_____

_____

_____

Imagine you were living in the 19th century and were suddenly transported to the present day. What do you imagine you would find most surprising?

_____

_____

_____

_____

What do you think would be most frightening?

_____

_____

What would be most amusing?

_____

_____

What would be most useful out of all the inventions in the 20th century?

_____

Listing Change

Write a list of things that change rapidly and a second list of things that change slowly.

Rapid change

_____

_____

_____

_____

_____

_____

_____

_____

_____

_____

Slow change

_____

_____

_____

_____

_____

_____

_____

_____

_____

_____

Write a list of things that change daily, for example, world population.

_____

_____

_____

_____

_____

_____

_____

_____

_____

List things that never change.

_____

_____

_____

_____

_____

_____

_____

_____

_____

_____

Buckets

List as many uses as you can for a bucket.

Stamp Out Poverty

World governments should abandon space travel and all money should be directed to help eliminate poverty throughout the world because one-quarter of the world's population is badly malnourished.

Examine the statement above. List all the positive and negative arguments and any questions that arise.

Positives	Negatives	Questions
_____	_____	_____
_____	_____	_____
_____	_____	_____
_____	_____	_____
_____	_____	_____
_____	_____	_____
_____	_____	_____
_____	_____	_____
_____	_____	_____

What decision(s) did you reach? Do you support the statement? _____

_____

_____

New and Improved

Design a new shower, and explain the reasons for any changes. You may like to use the BAR strategy to help decide on features that could be improved and ways of doing it. Illustrate your new shower design below.

B = make **bigger** or **smaller**

A = **add** something

R = **remove** something and **replace** it with something else

Change: _____

Reasons: _____

_____

Change: _____

Reasons: _____

_____

Change: _____

Reasons: _____

Before   **After**

What a Legend!

Describe a hero or heroine who is living at the present time. This can be a fictional person. Start with a physical description and then move beyond this to explain the other qualities he or she has. Think of 12 heroic tasks that he or she must complete.

Description of hero or heroine   **Explain the twelve heroic tasks.**

_____   1. _____

_____   2. _____

_____   3. _____

_____   4. _____

_____   5. _____

_____   6. _____

_____   7. _____

_____   8. _____

_____   9. _____

_____ 10. _____

_____ 11. _____

_____ 12. _____

You, as the hero, have to select three of the following objects to help with the tasks. Which would you choose and why would they be selected?

matches, jellybeans, a deck of cards, a rope, a skateboard, a magnifying glass, newspaper, a hat, a blanket, a boat, bicycle, a hammer, nails, money, shoes, soap, spoon, mirror, pocket knife, screwdriver, a spade

Choice   **Reasons**

_____   _____

_____   _____

_____   _____

Space Invention

Invent something unusual that can be used in space.

Suggestions: A feeding machine which can be used in a weightless environment, an alien-greeting robot, a space probe that can be sent out to analyze each new planet you approach.

Describe your invention in the squares below.

What it is	Description of components
How it works	**What it can be used for**
Special features	**Illustration**

Snow for Sale

Think of some innovative uses for snow.

Design an advertising campaign to sell snow.

_____

_____

_____

_____

_____

_____

_____

_____

_____

_____

_____

_____

_____

_____

Public Transportation

Brainstorm solutions for this problem:

People don't like using public transportation.

_____

_____

_____

_____

_____

_____

_____

_____

_____

_____

Improving Transportation

Choose one form of transportation. Improve this form so that it could move more people than at present and would be more comfortable for a long trip. Draw your new form of transportation and describe the improvements you have made.

Pyramids of Egypt

Below is a drawing of an Egyptian pyramid.

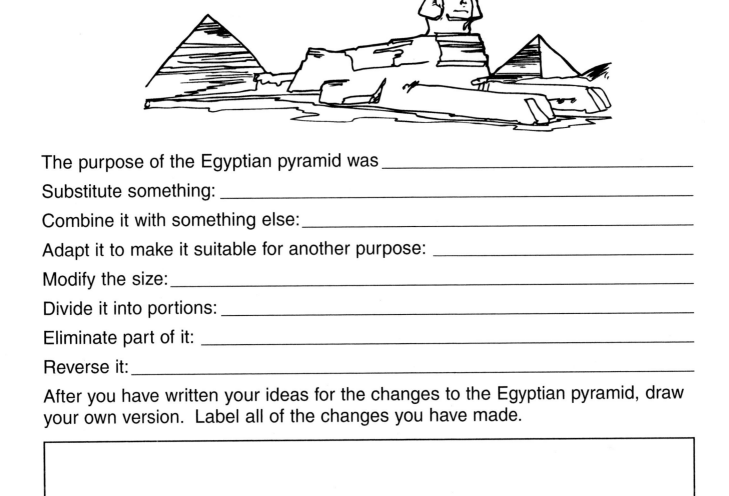

The purpose of the Egyptian pyramid was _____

Substitute something: _____

Combine it with something else: _____

Adapt it to make it suitable for another purpose: _____

Modify the size: _____

Divide it into portions: _____

Eliminate part of it: _____

Reverse it: _____

After you have written your ideas for the changes to the Egyptian pyramid, draw your own version. Label all of the changes you have made.

```



```

My new design is called _____

Its purpose is _____

Lunch Special

Organize a lunch special for your school cafeteria. Make sure that it tastes good and is healthful.

Describe and illustrate your meal in the box below.

Name of lunch special:	Illustration
Description: _____ _____ _____ _____ _____	

Design and produce an advertising poster for your lunch special.

Clothing

1. List six things that affect the type of clothing people wear and make a note of how each thing makes a difference to their choices.

Influence	How does it make a difference?
1.	
2.	
3.	
4.	
5.	
6.	

2. Quickly select five letters from the alphabet (do not include Q). Find an article of clothing beginning with each of these letters. In the table below, note what type of clothing it is, where it comes from, and who wears it.

Name of Item	What is it?	Where from?	Who wears it?
1.			
2.			
3.			
4.			
5.			

3. Now illustrate and label one of these articles of clothing.

Clothing *(cont.)*

1. Speaking of items of clothing, what do these expressions mean?

   Keep your shirt on:_____

   Treat her with kid gloves: _____

   If the shoe fits, wear it:_____

   He'd give you the shirt off his back: _____

2. How does climate affect the clothing you wear? Draw yourself sensibly dressed for the following conditions. Include any accessories you may also need.

Extremely hot	Extremely cold	Extremely wet	Extremely windy

Hats

1. List, draw, and label as many types of hats as you can. Show who wears the hat and where you'll find him or her (in which country).

2. Why are there so many different types of head coverings? Give as many reasons as you can.

_____

_____

_____

_____

_____

_____

_____

_____

Hats *(cont.)*

3. Make a hat for all occasions. Put your mind to work to create a useful hat that is also formal, sporty, protective, etc.

4. What do these hat expressions mean?

Keep it under your hat:_____

Throw your hat in the ring: _____

Pass the hat around: _____

Take your hat off to someone: _____

Scratch and Smell

List all of the ways you could be protected by your sense of smell. Now list all of the ways you could be protected by your sense of touch. Write about the importance of these two senses to the survival of human beings.

Mouth Watering!

Ponder this question and come up with as many answers as you can think of.

How can your sense of taste help you other than telling you that you like or dislike your food? Create a poster telling about the sense of taste and what it does.

Seeing is Believing!

What are some things that you have learned using:
- your sense of sight?
- your sense of hearing?

Draw a picture showing what you have learned.

Design with Numbers

Design a house floor plan. It must consist of four bedrooms, a kitchen, a living room, bathroom, laundry room, dining room, family room, and garage. Decide on the area of each room and the total area of the house.

Hidden Meanings

Explain the meaning of each box.

0 – 144!	TIME a b ⊠ d e	What Must
1. _____	5. _____	9. _____

Issue Issue Issue Issue Issue Issue Issue Issue Issue Issue	Knee Light	Me Quit!
2. _____	6. _____	10. _____

t h g i n	F R U S F R U S F R U S	F r i e n d s Standing ———— Miss F r i e n d s
3. _____	7. _____	11. _____

HIJKLMNO	B BA BACK	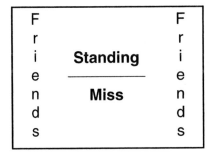
4. _____	8. _____	12. _____

Reverse Words

Reverse words are words that become different words when read backwards. Write the words and their reverses from the clues below. An example has been done for you.

physician/fish = doc/cod

1. sticky substance/rodent = _____

2. doodle/large hospital room = _____

3. cooking container/the best = _____

4. cat and dog/part of staircase = _____

5. not die/cruel = _____

6. not later/opposite of lost = _____

7. half of twenty/tennis court separation = _____

8. a belt/pieces = _____

9. flying mammals/knife injury = _____

10. pullout from a dresser/prize = _____

11. take a quick look/not give away = _____

12. baby rests/section of a bridge = _____

13. heavenly body/rodents = _____

14. takes skin off vegetables/nightly rest = _____

15. part of body/hair slicker = _____

Initializations and Acronyms

Acronyms are words formed from the initial letters of the words for which they stand. An example is VIP, which means "very important person." What do the following mean?

1. SWAK _____

2. HQ _____

3. RR _____

4. ERA _____

5. CPA _____

6. AWOL _____

7. TLC _____

8. GI _____

9. SOS _____

10. HEW _____

11. ASAP _____

12. PA _____

13. UFO _____

14. DJ _____

15. COD _____

Palindromes

Palindromes are words, phrases, sentences, or numbers that read the same forward and backward. Write a palindrome that relates to each word or phrase below. An example has been done for you.

Example: trick or joke = gag

1. midday _____

2. past tense of the verb *do* _____

3. a female sheep _____

4. robert's nickname _____

5. a small child _____

6. a little chick's noise _____

7. an organ of the body used for sight _____

8. a father's nickname _____

9. something that fails to work _____

10. the sound of a horn _____

11. something a baby wears _____

12. songs sung alone _____

13. a mother's nickname _____

14. an Eskimo canoe _____

15. even, flat _____

16. soda _____

17. a woman's name _____

18. a small dog _____

19. a brave or skillful act _____

20. relating to government or citizenship _____

Shipwrecked!

List three people you would like to be shipwrecked with and give reasons for your choices.

_____

_____

_____

_____

_____

List things you would need to retrieve from the ship to help in your survival.

_____

_____

_____

_____

_____

_____

_____

_____

The Amazing Hat

Design a hat that has at least four uses. Draw it here, and label the parts.

Describe how the hat works and for whom it would be useful.

_____

_____

_____

_____

_____

_____

_____

Progress Chart

Page	Title	Date	Completed

Progress Chart *(cont.)*

Page	Title	Date	Completed

Progress Chart *(cont.)*

Page	Title	Date	Completed

Progress Chart *(cont.)*

Page	Title	Date	Completed

Progress Chart *(cont.)*

Page	Title	Date	Completed

Progress Chart *(cont.)*

Page	Title	Date	Completed

Progress Chart *(cont.)*

Page	Title	Date	Completed

Progress Chart *(cont.)*

Page	Title	Date	Completed

Answer Key

Brain Warmups

Page 15
1. 27 animals
2. 300 students
3. Answers will vary. Samples:
   200+85
   2 hundreds, eight tens, and five ones
   15 x 19
   300–15

Page 16
Answers will vary.

Page 17
Answers will vary.

Page 18
7, 21, 49, 70, 77, 28
35, 70, 84, 21, 14
35, 42, 49, 70, 77
28, 14, 7, 14, 28
35, 77, 56, 35, 42
56, 63, 14, 49

Page 19
Across
1. 28
2. 18
3. 85
Down
1. 38
2. 88
3. 89
4. 48

Page 20
M-A-B-C-D-F-G-J-L-N-O-M

Page 21
12, 3, 15, 20, 14, 22, 2, 19, 8, 2, 12

Page 22
5 + 7 + 4 + 18 = 34

Page 23
C = 80 miles

Page 24
1. □
2. △
3. ○
4. ♡
5. ○
6. □
7. ◗
8. △
9. ♡
10. ▭

Page 25
△'s
sun
slide
swings
table
hills
O's
tree
fruit on tree
sun
slide
cup

Page 26
8 triangles

Page 27
Answers will vary.

Page 28
1. a. 50 students
   b. 4th grade
2. a. 98 kilometers
   b. no

Page 29
3. a. $284.95
   b. yes, $228.60
4. a. 7 team members
   b. 0

Page 30
5. a. $3.07
   b. $29.19
6. a. $37.36
   b. $34.64

Page 31
Bob Johnson, age 7
Bobby Wilson, age 8
Robert Anderson, age 9

Page 32
There are many answers. Some possible answers include the following:
1. h d
2. 2 q
3. 1 q, 2 d, 1 n
4. 1 q, 1 d, 3 n
5. 5 d
6. 10 n
7. 4 d, 2 n
8. 3 d, 4 n
9. 2 d, 6 n
10. 1 d, 8 n
11. 8 n, 10 p

Answer Key (cont.)

12. 6 n, 20 p
13. 4 n, 30 p
14. 2 n, 40 p
15. 1 n, 45 p
16. 10 p, 4 d
17. 20 p, 3 d
18. 30 p, 2 d
19. 40 p, 1 d
20. 50 p

Page 33

Ted Agee, age 9

Theodore Chin, age 8

Teddy Dalton, age 10

Page 34

Circle, triangle, square, rectangle

Shapes are fun.

Page 35

The safe way across is 60 ÷ 15, 16 kg x 4, 112 m + 36 m, 17 – 9 – 4, $4.20 – $3.80, 32 ÷ 8, 1 + 2 + 3 + 4 – 6, 10 + 3 – 9

Page 36

1. Fill the 5 L jug. Pour 3 L into the 3 L jug from the 5 L jug. Empty the 3 L jug. Pour 2 L from the 5 L jug into the now empty 3 L jug. Fill the 5 L jug. That makes 7 L.
2. 7 new walls
3. 1 + 2 = 3
   3 x 2 = 1
   1 x 3 = 3
   4 – 3 = 1
   3 + 3 = 1
   2 – 3 = 4

Page 37 and 38

Answers will vary.

Page 39

Straight letters: A, E, F, H, I, K, L, M, N, T, V, W, X, Y, Z

Curved letters: C, J, O, S, U

Both: B, D, G, P, Q, R

Page 40

Some examples: (there are many)

adult, alien, arise, atlas, drain, drier, easel, enter, erase, learn, lined, lunar, radar, rider, rinse, risen, ruled, ruler, rural, sinus, slate, slide, snail, stand, stare, steal, tease

Page 41

Do you promise to tell the tooth, the whole tooth, and nothing but the tooth?

Page 42

stars

spars

spare

space

Page 43

23 words: alone, Anne, lane, lean, leap, Leon, loan, lone, neon, Nepal, Noel, none, nope, opal, open, pale, pane, panel, peal, plan, plane, plea, pole

Page 44

1. DAD
2. BAGGAGE
3. DEAF
4. ACE

Page 45

33 words: ash, can, cap, has, hip, his, nap, nip, pan, pin, sap, sin, spa, cash, chap, chin, chip, hasp, Inca, inch, pain, scan, shin, ship, snip, span, spic, spin, chain, china, panic, Spain

Page 46

Names can be in any order:

Peter Pan

Roger Rabbit

Doctor Doolittle

Donald Duck

Mickey Mouse

Black Beauty

Miss Muffett

Goosey Gander

Mister McGregor

Tommy Tucker

Maid Marion

Page 47

rain, hail, cloud, fog

Page 48

Reading is lots of fun!

Page 49

1. hen pen
2. far star
3. hot pot
4. hare chair
5. ship trip
6. loose goose
7. best rest
8. mad dad
9. big wig
10. book nook
11. slow crow
12. lunch bunch
13. wet jet
14. nice mice
15. cat hat

Answer Key *(cont.)*

Page 50
1. job
2. mad
3. new
4. old
5. ill
6. all
7. car
8. fix
9. use
10. fat
11. end
12. boy
13. cat
14. say
15. try

Page 51
1. deep sleep
2. other brother
3. can Dan
4. large barge
5. bare hare
6. tall mall
7. wild child
8. peg leg
9. dome home
10. fish dish
11. eat meat
12. silly Billy
13. fat cat
14. rude dude
15. spare fare
16. brief grief
17. more score
18. old mold
19. sad dad
20. lazy daisy

Page 52
Here are 41 words:
3 letters: cod, cud, cue, die, doe, due, duo, ice, led, lid, lie, oil, old
4 letters: cell, clue, code, coil, cold, deli, dice, dole, duel, dull, iced, idle, idol, lied, loud, lull
5 letters: cello, cloud, could, lucid, oiled, oldie
6 letters: coiled, collie, docile, lolled, lulled
7 letters: collide

Page 53
Answers will vary.
Samples: came, ram, camera, rice, are, care, mice, race, ice, ear, ace, mace

Pages 54–71
Answers will vary.

Page 72
1. nose
2. ears
3. cannister
4. ball
5. ring
6. boat
7. wheel
8. lemon

Pages 73–83
Answers will vary.

Page 84
4 colors

Page 85
1. five (counting you and the driver)
2. plane

Page 86
1. stamp value
2. tree is reversed
3. seagull missing
4. coconuts have fallen
5. footprints
6. extra shark
7. one less perforation on the right side
8. sun has moved
9. a bottle
10. torn corner

Page 87
1. Turkey
2. New Zealand
3. Britain
4. Iran
5. France
6. Wales
7. Canada
8. Israel
9. Peru

Page 88
1. clocktower—different times
2. sun's position
3. clear sky/rain
4. birds/no birds
5. leaves on tree/no leaves
6. ducks on pond/no ducks
7. clean chair/newspaper and leaves on chair
8. different flowers
9. different paths to tower
10. empty trash can, trash on ground/full trash can

Answer Key (cont.)

Page 89
1. He couldn't sleep with the light on.
2. to become a light housekeeper
3. It's always waving.
4. Both crews were marooned.
5. and cargoes go in ships?
6. The spiral staircase drove him around the bend.
7. They beam all the time.
8. a nervous wreck

Page 90

B

Pages 91–93

Answers will vary.

Page 94
1. 26 letters in the alphabet
2. 52 cards in a deck
3. 88 piano keys
4. 3 blind mice (see how they run)
5. 4 quarts in a gallon
6. 11 players on a football team
7. 7 continents on the Earth
8. 50 states in the United States
9. 6 points for a touchdown
10. 20,000 leagues under the sea
11. 1,001 Arabian Nights
12. 5 digits in a zip code
13. 5 fingers on the right or left hand
14. 4 seasons in the year
15. 8 sides on a stop sign

Page 95

Answers will vary.

Page 96

No correct answer—if the joke is funny it must be right!

Pages 97–101

Answers will vary.

Brain Workouts

Page 103
1. 43 small holes
2. 576 onions
3. $10.76 each

Page 104
4. 855 holes
5. 14 bundles
6. 5 potatoes in each pot

Page 105
7. $7.11
8. 9 rows
9. $19.83
10. 264 apples

Pages 106–108

Answers will vary.

Page 109

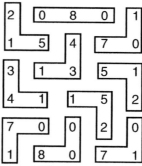

Page 110

Answers will vary.

Page 111
a. 6¢ change
b. 2 sackets of potatoes with 12¢ left

Page 112 and 113

Answers will vary.

Page 114
1. 490 km/hour
2. 5 cm/minute
3. 19 km/hour
4. 160 km/hour
5. 50 m/minute
6. 0.5 km/hour (It was being towed to the launch pad.)

Page 115

Phonograph—1877

Gramophone—1887

Tape recorder—1898

LP—1948

Cassette—1960

DAT—1970

CD—1980

DVD—1997

Page 116

1492 x 1

746 x 2

373 x 4

Page 117
1. (35 ÷ 5) x (27 ÷ 3) = 63
2. (32 ÷ 4) x (49 ÷ 7) = 56
3. (72 ÷ 9) x (24 ÷ 8) = 24
4. (56 ÷ 7) x (64 ÷ 8) = 64
5. (36 ÷ 6) x (35 ÷ 7) = 30

Page 118

Melanie—wolves, potato chips

Sarah—gorillas, hot dogs

Rachael—jaguars, lollipops

Jessica—ponies, chocolate bars

Answer Key (cont.)

Page 119

Answers will vary.

Page 120

Fat Chance, 8.9

Page 121

All have the lucky number three in them but 37 x 9 = 333 has three threes.

Page 122

Andre—letter, aunt, no stamp

Cindy—postcard, mom, pet stamp

Daphne—parcel, dad, flower stamp

Ben—bill, baker, building stamp

Page 123

Page 124

Abigail won, then Bernard, Cathryn, Denise, Edward, Francis, Gabby

Page 125

1. duck
2. penguin
3. pelican
4. swan
5. gull
6. goose
7. loon
8. crane
9. egret
10. sandpiper

Pages 126 and 127

Clue 1: steel

Clue 2: sharp

Clue 3: joins

Clue 4: wood

Clue 5: hammer

What's in the bag? a nail

Pages 128 and 129

Clue 1: scales

Clue 2: slither

Clue 3: coils

Clue 4: long

Clue 5: molt

What's in the bag? a snake

Pages 130 and 131

Clue 1: strange

Clue 2: aircraft

Clue 3: hovers

Clue 4: mystery

Clue 5: light

What's in the bag? a U.F.O.

Pages 132 and 133

Clue 1: chewy

Clue 2: dough

Clue 3: baked

Clue 4: sugary

Clue 5: dozens

What's in the bag? cookies

Page 134

1. Alan
2. Anne
3. Arab
4. band
5. bank
6. bran
7. barn
8. nana

   Extra Points: bandana

Page 135

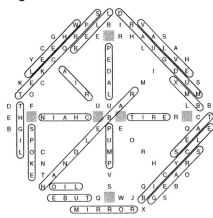

Page 136

Ideograph

Page 137

1. duo
2. duet
3. dual
4. couple
5. couplet
6. pair
7. two
8. twosome
9. deuce

Page 138

1. farms
2. grams
3. harms
4. crams
5. marsh
6. roams
7. warms
8. ramps
9. reams
10. smart

Answer Key (cont.)

Page 139

The Complete Angler

Page 140

1. beats
2. teary
3. swear
4. artsy
5. strew
6. beast
7. waste
8. retry
9. water
10. yeast

Page 141

1. tomato
2. olive
3. elderberry
4. yam
5. mango
6. onion
7. nectarine
8. eggplant

Page 142

cars
oars
ours
furs
firs
fire
file
film

Page 143

Order of answers may vary: buzzard, cardinal, chicken, cormorant, eagle, ostrich, parrot, pigeon, sparrow, vulture, woodpecker

Page 144

Persephone

Page 145

Catherine of Aragon
Anne Boleyn
Jane Seymour
Anne of Cleves
Catherine Howard
Catherine Parr

Page 146

sand
sank
dank
dane
done
dune
dune
june
jane
sane
sand

Page 147

1. ice skating
2. pewter
3. spoon
4. stocks
5. dugout
6. bayberry
7. samplers
8. peddlers
9. linen
10. trencher
11. dame school
12. indigo
13. linseed
14. lye
15. quoits
16. hornbook
17. doublet
18. johnnycake
19. saltbox
20. sabbath

Page 148

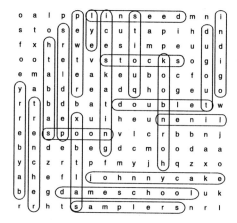

Page 149

Answers will vary.

Page 150

1. pinch
2. pink
3. pint
4. pinball
5. Ping-Pong
6. pinnacle
7. pineapple
8. pinpoint
9. pin cushion

Page 151

mint
candy
toffee
popcorn
licorice
chocolate
chewing gum
marshmallow
butterscotch

Answer Key *(cont.)*

Pages 152–178
Answers will vary.

Page 179
T
T
F
F

Pages 180–183
Answers will vary.

Page 184
1. England
2. France
3. Italy
4. Egypt
5. U.S.A.
6. England
7. France
8. Australia
9. India
10. Japan

Page 185
Old Tom

Page 186
1. What you see is what you get.
2. before
3. tonight
4. easy
5. because
6. grin
7. sigh
8. thanks
9. rolling on the floor laughing
10. on the other hand
11. long time no see
12. by the way
13. see you

Page 187
Last weeks charts:
1. That'll Be the Day
2. Da Doo Ron Ron
3. Love Potion No. 9
4. Peggy Sue
5. Run Around Sue
6. Heartbreak Hotel
7. Shakin' All Over
8. Rock Around the Clock
9. Wild One
10. Shake, Rattle 'n Roll

Page 188
Answers will vary.

Page 189
1. late date
2. fat rat
3. bad lad
4. rude dude
5. bug's mug
6. long song
7. fat cat
8. double trouble
9. big pig
10. Swiss miss
11. bony pony
12. bright light
13. funny bunny
14. glad lad
15. lazy daisy
16. sad dad
17. mouse house
18. no dough
19. cross boss
20. funny money

Page 190
1. 16
2. 15
3. 25
4. J
5. W
6. U
7.   8.
9. IX
10. sheep

Page 191
It was daylight and the Express driver could see him.

Page 192
Answers will vary.

Page 193
1. scatterbrained
2. six feet below the ground
3. a square meal
4. neon light
5. little league
6. big man on campus
7. pain in the neck
8. check up
9. Tiny Tim
10. once over lightly
11. keep it under your hat
12. high school

Answer Key *(cont.)*

Page 194

The house burned down, and the firefighters tried to save it.

Page 195

Answers will vary.

Brain Challenges

Page 197

Answers will vary.

Page 198

1. 9 m x 3 m = 30 bricks x 20 bricks = 600 bricks
2. 40 km x 3 m = 133,333 bricks x 20 bricks = 2,666,660
3. 40,000 m x 3 m = 120,000 m²
4. 2,666,660 bricks x $585 = $1,559,996,100
5. 2,666,660 x 10 cm = 266,666 m
6. 2,666,660 x 3.5 kg = 9,333,310 kg

Page 199

140 km long

Page 200

1. 16
2. 8
3. B: the orbit takes longer, must be higher
4. A: 10:30 A.M.
   B: 12 noon
5. night—it's on the opposite side of the world
6. 8 times a day
7. the earth

Page 201

1. no
2. yes
3. yes
4. yes
5. no
6. yes
7. no
8. yes
9. yes
10. no

Page 202

French: dix, neuf, huit, sept, six, cinq, quatre, trois, deux, un, zero

Spanish: diez, nueve, ocho, siete, seis, cinco, cuatro, tres, dos, uno, cero

Page 203

1. James Bond
2. 7
3. 10
   20
   100
   1,000

4. 52
5. a plane
6. a. Jules Verne
   b. Jules Verne
   c. George Orwell
7. Answers will vary.

Pages 204–207

Answers will vary.

Page 209

Day 59

Page 210

One possible answer is: 99 + 999 + 9 + 9 + 9 = 1,125

Page 211

Answers will vary.

Page 212

0, 1, 1 ,2, 3, 5, 8, 13, 21, 34, 55, 89, 144, 233

rule: add the last two numbers to get the next number.

Page 213

Answers will vary.

Page 214

Shari bought the shorts for $25.
Rhonda bought the dress for $30.
Jenna bought the skirt for $20.
Margaret bought the shirt for $11.

Page 215

Answers will vary.

Page 216

Answers will vary.

Page 217

Cart 1: 165 + 100 + 100 + 200 + 400 = $965
Cart 2: 25 + 150 + 160 + 250 + 500 = $1,085
Cart 3: 130 + 80 + 160 + 200 + 400 = $970
Cart 4: 55 + 120 + 240 + 250 + 500 = $1,165
Cart 4 won

Page 218

	A	B	C	
A	2	4	8	14
B	3	5	7	15
C	9	6	1	16
	14	15	16	

Page 219

28 handshakes

Extension: Answers will vary.

Pages 220 and 221

Clue 1: padded
Clue 2: heals
Clue 3: injury
Clue 4: sticky
Clue 5: strip
What's in the bag: a bandaid

Answer Key (cont.)

Pages 222 and 223

Clue 1: gadget

Clue 2: viewer

Clue 3: channels

Clue 4: operates

Clue 5: T.V.

What's in the bag: a remote control

Pages 224 and 225

Clue 1: private

Clue 2: ears

Clue 3: carries

Clue 4: music

Clue 5: clamp

What's in the bag: headphones

Pages 226 and 227

Clue 1: handle

Clue 2: smack

Clue 3: winged

Clue 4: insect

Clue 5: hit

What's in the bag: a flyswatter

Page 228

put-off

defer

postpone

discontinue

linger

detain

arrest

stall

impede

hinder

dawdle

stay

loiter

overlook

suspend

Page 229

blunt

brunt

grunt

grant

grand

brand

bland

blank

plank

plant

slant

shan't

Shane

share

sharp

Page 230

Page 231

Answers will vary.

Page 232

1. blues
2. hip hop
3. disco
4. rock
5. country
6. folk
7. pop
8. rock and roll
9. classical
10. techno
11. heavy metal
12. punk

Page 233

Boogie Woogie, Jump Blues, Doo Wop, Honky Tonk

Page 234

electricity

capability

stability

minority

gravity

activity

longevity

likability

sensitivity

Page 235

1. cabin
2. galley
3. port
4. stern
5. hull
6. bow
7. rats
8. anchor
9. engine

Answer Key (cont.)

10. starboard

Capehorner

Page 236

bauble

bubble

hubble

rubble

clubbed

quibble

bluebeard

bubblegum

Page 237

cone

consent

console

contain

content

contest

constant

consonant

continent

Page 238

tribute

brunette

buttress

rebutton

turbo-jet

briquette

buttercup

litterbug

jitterbug

gettysburg

Page 239

1. Bloomers Rd.
2. Mangrove Rd.
3. Customer Rd.
4. Employer Rd.
5. Composer Rd.
6. Enormous Rd.
7. Compared Rd.
8. Geometry Rd.

Page 240

1. dandelion
2. acid rain
3. airline
4. drive-in
5. radio
6. radial
7. cradle
8. arcade

9. alien
10. video

(word whose letters are found in Leonardo Da Vinci)

Pages 241–242

Answers will vary.

Page 243

1. guide—lead
2. accordian—wind instrument
3. scramble—mix up
4. aqueduct—water channel
5. suffix—word ending
6. chess—game
7. pawn—chess piece
8. survey—look over
9. excerpt—passage from a book
10. scorpion—poisonous animal
11. zither—string instrument
12. junk—trash

Page 244

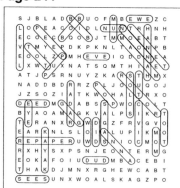

Page 245

1. Q
2. XTC
3. NME
4. NV
5. B, D, K, or L
6. O
7. SA
8. FX
9. J
10. CU
11. AT
12. T
13. G or O
14. XL
15. DK

Answer Key (cont.)

Page 246

output

turnout

untruth

butter up

outburst

Timbuktu

truthful

about-turn

buttercup

out of tune

Page 247

tale

travel

elevator

overeat

revote

voter

over

rev

Page 248

conduct

Pages 249–254

Answers will vary.

Page 255

1. New York
2. Kuwait
3. Tokyo
4. Oslo
5. Ottawa
6. Athens
7. Seoul
8. London

Page 256

1. South Entrance
2. bridge, ropes, lion, bomb, building, bus, water

Page 257

parrot   gazelle

cheetah   rhinoceros

condor   turtle

crocodile   whale

elephant   woodpecker

Pages 258–278

Answers will vary.

Page 279

1. O Gross!
2. Tennis Shoes or 10 issues
3. Night falls
4. H_2O

5. Long Time No See
6. Neon Light
7. Surfs Up
8. Quarterback, Halfback, Fullback
9. What goes up must come down
10. Quit following me
11. Misunderstanding between friends
12. Matinee

Page 280

1. tar/rat
2. draw/ward
3. pot/top
4. pets/step
5. live/evil
6. now/won
7. ten/net
8. strap/parts
9. bats/stab
10. drawer/reward
11. peek/keep
12. naps/span
13. star/rats
14. peels/sleep
15. leg/gel

Page 281

1. Sealed With a Kiss
2. Headquarters
3. Railroad
4. Equal Rights Amendment
5. Certified Public Accountant
6. Absent Without Leave
7. Tender Loving Care
8. Government Issue
9. Save Our Ship
10. Health, Education, and Welfare
11. As Soon as Possible
12. Public Address
13. Unidentified Flying Object
14. Disc Jockey
15. Cash on Delivery

Page 282

1. noon
2. did
3. ewe
4. Bob
5. tot
6. peep
7. eye
8. pop or dad
9. dud
10. toot
11. bib
12. solos
13. mom or mum
14. kayak
15. level
16. pop
17. Answers will vary. They include Anna, Eve, Hannah, and Nan.
18. pup
19. deed
20. civic

Pages 283 and 284

Answers will vary.

Super Solver Award

To: _____

From: _____

Date: _____

Super Solver Award

To: _____

From: _____

Date: _____